"We're all looking for relationships that go beyond the surface and delve into the heart—we want to be known and know others. However, often we hide who we truly are, in fear and shame, concerned that our lives aren't as picture-perfect as our friends' social media stories. In *Real*, Catherine Parks writes with warmth and insight, inviting us out of the shadows of our sin and into the mercy of Jesus."

**Melissa Kruger, TGC blogger; author of *In All Things:
A Nine-Week Devotional Bible Study on Unshakeable Joy***

"In this superb and timely book, Catherine Parks encourages us to pursue friendships that go beyond nod-along pity parties. In our day, there is much talk of authenticity and being 'real'. Catherine points us toward true, mutual vulnerability, not as an end in itself, but rather, as a means of journeying together back to the cross of Christ. This book has transformed the way I view what friendship is and what it is ultimately for."

**Rachel Wilson, co-author of *The Life You Never Expected***

"I'll tell anyone anything, as long as I'm not face to face with them. Being real is easy when I don't have to look a person in the eyes while I confess my sin or address their sin, confess my fears or speak lovingly to their fears—and I fear I'm not alone in this. Catherine Parks gets real with her readers about her own reticence in being real, helping us to see that our real problem is with God."

**Lore Ferguson Wilbert, writer at Sayable.net**

"A deeply perceptive account of how to live real life—in the only way that matters."

**Dr Kirsten Birkett, Dean of Women, Oak Hill College,
London; author of *The Essence of the Reformation***

"God has woven into our being the desire for deep relationships where we are known, seen, understood, and loved. In an age of timelines that function as highlight reels and of perfectly edited selfies, the very thing we were created for often feels far off. Catherine masterfully teaches that repentance before God and acceptance of his forgiveness precede intimate spiritual fellowship with others. *Real* is a timely read for those desiring to know God more deeply and longing to be more fully known by others."

**Shar Walker, Regional Women's Director,
Campus Outreach Lynchburg; contributing author in
*Joyfully Spreading the Word***

"Most of us have multiple 'selves' that we put on display—almost like actors on a stage—depending upon the setting in which we find ourselves. We have a work self, a family self, a social gathering self, a church self, and so many other selves, all designed to control what other people think about us. Meanwhile, the gospel is right there, gently reminding us that we are already approved of in Jesus, and quietly beckoning us to stop our posing, and instead offer others the gift of knowing us more truly and fully. In *Real*, Catherine has done a wonderful job of leading us in this direction, and so toward a more genuine experience of God and community. I highly recommend this book."

**Scott Sauls, Pastor, Christ Presbyterian Church,
Nashville, TN; author of *Jesus Outside the Lines*,
*Befriend*, and *From Weakness to Strength***

"This book moved me, changed me, showed me my need of the cross and inspired me to share this with others. A rare find—I couldn't put it down, was sad when it finished and will be coming back to it regularly to reveal afresh my sin and my need of a saviour. Catherine is ruthless in stripping back the layers to get to the root of our lack of real repentance, and immensely practical about what true repentance entails. I found myself genuinely confessing the heart of my sin, and therefore seeing real behaviour change. Catherine then brilliantly inspires us to do this in real relationships with others."

**Linda Allcock, London Women's Convention**

"Friendships are one of God's great gifts to us. In Christ, friendships are even more meaningful. God uses fellow believers to help us fight sin and persevere in faith. Yet, one of the great hindrances to true fellowship between believers is our propensity toward prideful pretending. We want others to think we have it all together when we really don't. In *Real*, Catherine shows us why we hide behind our masks, and how believing the gospel helps us to take them off. By repenting together, true fellowship is produced because we are free to see and enjoy God's grace in each other's lives. If you're looking for help in cutting through the fluff of superficial relationships, grab a group of sisters and spend time reading, praying, and applying this book."

**Garrett Kell, Lead Pastor, Del Ray Baptist Church,
Alexandria, VA**

"This book is really helpful in showing us why we will only be able to grow in our relationships with each other as we are honest about the heart issues beneath our surface sins and then come to God in repentance and faith. I realised as I read how much I am missing out by holding back in relationships that are a precious gift from the Lord and a huge opportunity for us to help each other grow more like Jesus. All Catherine says is rooted in God's word, she writes with great warmth and honesty, and her joy and delight at wanting to share this wonderful secret she has discovered is very evident."

**Andrea Trevenna, Associate Minister for Women,
St Nicholas Church, Sevenoaks, UK;
author of *The Heart of Singleness***

"In this wonderfully practical book, Catherine shows us what a difference it makes to our relationships when we drop the pretence, humbly admit our sins, and through temptation and failure keep pointing one another to our faithful Saviour, Jesus Christ."

**Sarah Hall, Women's Worker,
Emmanuel Church Wimbledon, UK**

CATHERINE PARKS

*Real*

thegoodbook
COMPANY

*For Mom and Dad,*
*who taught me the joy and grace of forgiveness.*

*And for Amber,*
*who patiently loved me and waited for me to get real.*
*Your friendship is one of God's kindest gifts to me.*

Real: The Surprising Secret to Deeper Relationships
© Catherine Parks/The Good Book Company, 2018

Published by:
The Good Book Company

Tel (US): 866 244 2165
Tel (UK): 0333 123 0880
Email (US): info@thegoodbook.com
Email (UK): info@thegoodbook.co.uk

Websites:
North America: www.thegoodbook.com
UK: www.thegoodbook.co.uk
Australia: www.thegoodbook.com.au
New Zealand: www.thegoodbook.co.nz

ISBN: 9781784982959 | Printed in the UK

Design by André Parker

# CONTENTS

# FOREWORD

*by Trillia Newbell*

*I*'ve always had a sensitive conscience: even before I became a Christian, I would confess wrongdoing to my parents. Vulnerability was never difficult for me when I was younger.

Oddly, once I became a Christian, I started to become more aware of how I would be viewed by others, and that vulnerability all of a sudden felt much more risky. I was 22 and wanted to be accepted. But God was gracious to me and gave me two friends, two accountability partners, two people serious about God and eager for true and honest fellowship.

My two close friends and I did accountability consistently for several years (and even to this day, one of them and I will catch up as if those college and single years aren't long gone). We would meet every other Friday afternoon. Our times together would consist of eating spaghetti, confession, encouragement, and prayers. We cried and laughed and shared the most intimate parts of ourselves. We were honest and open, often sharing things that might even make one blush with embarrassment.

Those formative years in my Christian walk were priceless. I learned the gift that is repentance and that I could bring anything before my heavenly Father. God was and remains incredibly approachable to me, because I know that if I confess my sin, he is faithful and just to forgive me and purify me (1 John 1 v 9). I know that I can come before his throne of grace and receive mercy and help in my time of need (Hebrews 4 v 16).

God also used those relationships to solidify my view of the church as a family. I knew that my friends and I weren't simply three girls pouring out our hearts to one another. We were, and still are, sisters—co-heirs with Christ! Relationships in the church are essential for our walk with him. I know this because there were times when I wasn't sure if I could walk the walk of faith. God used those relationships to keep me from wandering off course. Those sisters were in the race, in the fight, or—as my friend Catherine Parks has written here—on my team.

Those college friendships expanded beyond college into our single years and then through the beginning of our marriages. But as many of our stories go, two of us ended up moving away, beginning a search for new, deep relationships in our new homes.

In walks Catherine.

When I moved to the Nashville area, I knew that the only way for me to truly settle in and make our new location feel like home was to (1) find a church and commit to it and (2) find some friends and begin to build deep and true relationships. The Lord was faithful in both cases. I had known of Catherine Parks via her online articles and book. I reached out to her to see if we could meet up, and it was one of the best decisions I could have made.

Catherine and I hit it off quickly and easily. I don't remember all that we talked about, but I do remember going from "Nice to meet you" to "Let's confess our sins" within a matter of a few hangouts (it may have even been our first!). I'm not good with surface-level conversations, so I dove right in. It was something I was used to; but it wasn't necessarily Catherine's default. Yet she made sure to let me know that for her, it was good and challenging to think beyond the surface and resist the urge to give coined answers of "I'm fine."

I share this with you because I am both a reader and an author. As a reader, I want to know that the author is authentic and can write with at least a measure of authority on the topic; and as I'm a Christian reader, it's even more assuring when I know that the author has integrity. Catherine has walked out and wrestled with the truth that she writes about in *Real*. She isn't writing from a place of superiority or as someone who has arrived. Rather, Catherine is a fellow sojourner in the faith, on a mission to finish the race well. Confession, repentance, and being real are essential in that goal.

In *Real* you will find wise counsel, biblical exposition, and personal stories that will inspire, encourage, and challenge you as you seek to be honest with yourself and with those around you. We will learn the futility of chasing after what we think we want versus the value of chasing after what is right. We will learn to face our sin for what it is. No excuses. No defending.

But Catherine doesn't leave us to wallow in condemnation and self-pity. That isn't the point of confession, nor is it the goal of repentance. It is indeed God's kindness that leads us to repentance (Romans 2 v 4). God's word tells us that if we confess our sin, God is faithful and just to forgive us (1 John 1 v 9). We can trust that God will do as he says—he meets our sin with forgiveness and grace. As Catherine has written, "When we're assured of our Father's forgiveness, instead of covering up in front of others, we can confess—be honest about our sin" (p 31).

We will never outgrow this message of grace and repentance. And we will never outgrow our need for one another. Whether you have a core group of friends who are thriving and already committed to seeking Jesus together, or the concept of confession is absolutely new to you, this book is for you. Anyone at any stage will benefit from the pages ahead.

**Trillia Newbell**
Author of *God's Very Good Idea* and *Fear and Faith*

# INTRODUCTION

*B*efore we begin, I really want you to get to know me.

I'm successful.

I'm intelligent.

I am a wise and self-sufficient woman.

In other words… I don't want you to know me at all. Not the real me. I only want you to get to know a carefully crafted version of me.

This has been my problem for as long as I can remember. I've spent a lifetime mastering the art of managing perceptions. I've learned to hide certain things about myself and to highlight others. Why? So that you'll like me. So that you'll be impressed by me. So that you'll want to be friends with me.

As a child, my shelves were lined with Bible memorization trophies and academic awards. I wanted people to know I was smart. As I grew older, rather than displaying awards, I walked around with the title of a book facing outward so that people could see I wasn't just reading a "beach read," but something weighty and important. That was how much I cared about what other people thought of me.

But I've come to suspect that I've been short-changing myself all along. And here's why.

Thirteen years ago, I was a newly married 23-year-old in a new city. My husband and I started attending a church, and Amber, a girl from our new small group, invited me to lunch one day. We quickly became friends and would often get together for dinner.

It was nice to have someone to hang out and laugh with. But to be honest, I thought Amber needed me more than I needed her. She would tell me her problems, and I would try to fix them. (Note: This is *not* what verbal processors want. I learned this the hard way.) But I rarely reciprocated in being honest about my own struggles to her—and there were definitely plenty of *those*.

Why all the hiding? Because I wanted to be friends with Amber, but at the same time I wanted to be the one who had it all together. I wanted depth without opening up. I wanted closeness while keeping my distance.

So I kept Amber at arm's length for years. And all the while I was pushing away the thing that I wanted most of all: a real relationship. This is the other desire that has motivated me for decades. Deep down, I long for the kind of friendships where I can let down my guard and not have to manage perceptions. I want to be truly who I am—to laugh with abandon, cry without embarrassment, and confess fears and failures. I long to be able to be honest and real and be loved unconditionally despite all the mess. And the irony is that I went about trying to build those relationships by hiding the mess, managing perceptions, and covering up my failings. Amber was just one of a long line of people to whom I refused to show the real me.

But over time, something changed. Gradually I *did* start to find the deeper relationships I was longing for.

And it didn't happen in the way I expected.

The secret to deeper relationships definitely wasn't in managing other people's perceptions of me.

It wasn't in learning to love myself, either—as if the mess inside me is really somehow beautiful. Contrary to what conventional wisdom sometimes tells us, I can't find freedom in accepting myself just the way I am and expecting others to do the same.

Instead, the secret to deeper relationships was simply in learning to be… real. Yes, real with myself. Yes, real with others. But most fundamentally, real with God. There's so much joy and freedom to be found in honest relationship with him. For me, that has meant developing an often-neglected biblical habit: repentance. Instead of hiding my flaws or trying to love myself in spite of them, I regularly bring them to the One who can take care of them completely.

The surprising secret to enjoying real relationships with those we know is to practice real repentance with the God we love.

That's the key that opens us up and allows us to invite others in.

That's the gateway to the friendships we're longing for.

So that's what we're going to explore in this book. Will you join me on this journey? It's a journey away from fake smiles and keeping up appearances, and towards a relationship with God where you get real with him so you can be real with others. I hope you'll grab a friend to join you, and I pray God uses this book to bring you real joy and real relationships.

# 1. FINSTA AND RINSTA

*I*t was the revolution that changed the way we communicate forever.

I graduated from college before the social-media and smartphone booms hit. Few of my friends had cell phones. Instead, we stayed up late, prank calling other students using the official phone directory, which listed each person's dorm landline number under his or her picture (it was nicknamed the "ugly book" for its less-than-flattering photos).

We had to leave each other notes on whiteboards outside our dorm rooms to let our roommates know where we were. We took pictures on film and had to have them printed at Walmart. When a friend went on a first date, rather than receiving text updates during the event, we all stayed up to hear every detail when she returned. Although we didn't have the technology to be constantly connected, we witnessed the details of each other's lives up close.

This idea of seeing the whole of a person—the good, the bad and the ugly in 360 degrees—is what makes relationships meaningful. The 2004 film *Shall We Dance?* tells the story of a middle-aged man who grows dissatisfied and takes up ballroom dancing to inject a spark into his life. In a pivotal scene, his wife discovers his secret hobby, and expresses her hurt:

> *We need a witness to our lives. There's a billion people on the planet—what does any one life really mean? But in a marriage, you're promising to care about everything. The good things, the bad things, the terrible things, the mundane things, all of it, all of the time, every day. You're saying, "Your life will not go unnoticed because I will notice it. Your life will not go unwitnessed because I will be your witness."*

If you're anything like me, you read a quote like that and find yourself longing for those kinds of deep relationships. And not just within marriage—this beautiful image of sharing our lives and being witnesses to what happens to one another is a picture of the kinds of deep relationships we were all created to enjoy with friends as well as family. We were made for relationships in which we are fully seen, fully understood, fully cared for, and fully loved.

In our current social-media age, most of us have more "witnesses" to our lives than ever. I can post a picture of myself at this moment, writing this book while eating Maniac's fried chicken in Franklin, Tennessee, and instantly people all over the world will know exactly what I'm doing. I can give family in Europe or Asia a play-by-play of my day, or livestream a child's sporting event. And this isn't reserved for close friends and family. People I have never met in person are witnesses to my life.

The problem is, these online "witnesses" don't see the whole picture. This is a public face—and most of us have one.

A few years ago I read the terms "finsta" and "rinsta" in an article about teenage girls and social media. Because teens and college students have been taught to protect their "brands," and because what they see on high-profile social-media accounts is so carefully curated, they develop two Instagram accounts—the finsta, or "fake Insta" account, and the rinsta, or "real Insta." One is hidden under a pseudonym, visible only to those let into the inner circle. This account with the real photos under a fake name is called the "finsta"— the fake account. The "rinsta" is the one visible to anyone, under a real name but with photos meticulously curated to share only the ideal image of the user. It's anything but real.

Even if you only have one account, Instagram and other social-media platforms have become places of comparison and frustration for many of us. If we're all curating our profiles, what we're actually witnessing is not each other's lives, but instead the picture-perfect highlights.

But this is not really a new phenomenon. I may not have grown up with social media, but I quickly learned how to fake that things were okay. Most kids learn the difference between "angry mom" and "phone mom." I used to think it was an amazing talent—one minute my mom was expressing her extreme frustration with my disobedience, only for me to be saved by the ring of the kitchen phone. She wouldn't miss a beat, talking to me all the way to the phone, stopping mid-word to say, "Hello?" in the sweetest voice I had ever heard. A rookie might think, "Oh good, she's not mad anymore." But one look at her eyes said otherwise. She could talk with concern and kindness while her eyes were saying, "I'm not done with you."

Now, I don't really think this was my mom being fake. She just did what she had to do. She didn't have the benefit of texting someone to say, "I'll call you back when my kids stop beating each other."

Now I teach my own kids something similar on the way to church—and if you're a parent, maybe you've played out this scene too: we're angry and impatient on the drive over, but the moment we step out of the car and into the building, our smiles are fixed and our responses prepared.

We all long for witnesses—but we desperately want to control what they see.

## FAKING OR FELLOWSHIP?

So if we long for connection and community, why do we so often default to fakery? It's because being real requires something that most of us find excruciatingly difficult: vulnerability. We don't want other people to see our emotional weak spots. In fact, this is why we often find online community easier—it gives us a defensive barrier to full exposure. Both online and offline, we've become experts at hiding the "real" us—and lots of us aren't sure how to stop.

It seems that it's getting harder to start building real relationships. My college friends knew the real me because they saw me pressed by all-nighters, boy problems, exam stress, and the physical effects of a hard volleyball season. The real Catherine was unavoidable in those moments. I couldn't hide my flaws or my pain, my joy or my sorrow. They shared in it all with me. And I shared in their lives in the same way.

Yet this was in some ways an artificial experience. I don't get to pull all-nighters with Abigail in the mildewed halls of Long Dorm anymore. I don't have long road trips in the volleyball van with Randi, Becca, Laura, and Anna. And while Jen is now my sister-in-law, she lives on the other side of the world instead of the other side of the shared-suite bathroom.

After college I got married, moved to a new city, and started over with relationships. And it wasn't nearly as easy as it had been in college. I was working full-time and didn't quite have the capacity for all-night soul-baring that I'd once had. I quickly discovered community in the real world wasn't quite so easy to come by. And even though I had always seen myself as independent, not really needing to share my heart with others, I gradually came to realize that even I longed to be seen and known—the innate human desire for true communion, a bond we might call "fellowship."

I grew up in churches in the American South, where the word "fellowship" had a certain connotation. Usually it was something we went to, as in "Mom's going to fry some chicken for the church fellowship." You might walk around and have the same conversation with twelve different people between second and third servings of banana pudding. These times of "fellowship" were great opportunities to meet new people, share a southern feast, and find out about other church members' weeks. But they didn't exactly demonstrate the meaning of the biblical term "fellowship," or *koinonia* in the Greek.

*Koinonia* is an intimate, spiritual fellowship. It's a communal bond. This fellowship starts with God— the holy Trinity of Father, Son, and Spirit united in perfect love. Creation is an overflow of this love; it flows from God's desire to share this fellowship with created human beings, made in the image of their Creator. This means that you and I were created with a fundamental desire for this kind of fellowship—we've been designed to enjoy a deep, spiritual relationship of love with God and with one another. It's the kind of relationship we glimpse briefly in Genesis chapters 1 and 2 as Adam and Eve walk and talk together in the Garden of Eden with God.

Humans have desired that same kind of fellowship ever since—and while God is the only One who can truly satisfy that desire, it's often in our human relationships that we first detect the lack. Researcher and best-selling author Brené Brown wrote that the "surest thing" she discovered in years of social work and research is this: "Connection is why we're here. We are hardwired to connect with others, it's what gives purpose and meaning to our lives, and without it there is suffering" (*Daring Greatly*). We don't just desire it; we actually need it. A study conducted by researchers at Brigham Young University over the course of 34 years, and involving more than 3 million participants, showed that social isolation and loneliness contributed to an average of 29% and 26% increased likelihood of mortality respectively. These statistics put the health risks of isolation and loneliness on a par with obesity. On the flipside, the existence of strong social relationships was observed to provide positive health benefits.

So let me ask you: do you have those kinds of relationships of intimate, spiritual fellowship? Maybe as you're reading this, you feel that fellowship is for other people, but you're too broken or too much of an outsider to have it. Or maybe you believed you had a good community of friends, but you're starting to question whether your relationships can be described by the term *koinonia.* You have plenty of surface-level friendships, but few if any of these deeper relationships. Or maybe you're like I've been in the past, and you just don't really think you need that kind of friendship.

Wherever you find yourself, know this: we're created for fellowship—and over the course of this book, we're going to work at growing it.

## THE GIFT OF FELLOWSHIP

So if we're made for this kind of deep fellowship, why do we not have it? Why do things often feel so shallow?

Because all of us are too busy hiding. As on social media, so throughout life our tendency is to cover up our true selves, rather than being honest and vulnerable about our weaknesses and failings. We present an image of having it all together and being able to do it all, while secretly feeling we might sink due to the weight of all our busyness. We're far quicker to tell friends about a success—the promotion, our child's milestone, a running distance—than a failure—that small dishonesty said to save face, the gossip we passed on about a co-worker, the lack of control over our anger with our children. Honesty feels too risky—what would people think of me if they knew?

But the root of the problem goes deeper. Real fellowship is a gift to us from the triune God, who made us in his image—which means that we can't experience this true fellowship with others unless we have fellowship with him.

And the thing that gets in the way of this fellowship with God is the same thing that hinders our fellowship with others. The Bible uses a short, blunt word to describe it: sin. For instance, here's 1 John 1 v 5 – 2 v 1:

*This is the message we have heard from him and declare to you: God is light; in him there is no darkness at all. If we claim to have fellowship with him and yet walk in the darkness, we lie and do not live out the truth. But if we walk in the light, as he is in the light, we have fellowship with one another, and the blood of Jesus, his Son, purifies us from all sin.*

*If we claim to be without sin, we deceive ourselves and the truth is not in us. If we confess our sins, he is faithful and just and will forgive us our sins and purify us from all unrighteousness. If we claim we have not sinned, we make him out to be a liar and his word is not in us.*

*My dear children, I write this to you so that you will not sin. But if anybody does sin, we have an advocate with the Father—Jesus Christ, the Righteous One.*

### #1 COVER UP

When it comes to our sin, John says that we can do one of two things with it before God: either confess it or cover it up.

Our natural response is to do the latter, from the Garden of Eden onwards. We'll see in the next chapter that after Adam and Eve sinned, they attempted to hide from God and used fig leaves in a futile effort to cover up their nakedness—and our human response today is likewise to hide and cover our shame. But John says that this has dangerous results.

First, "if we claim to be without sin, we deceive ourselves" (v 8). It's easy to fool ourselves into thinking that we're really not that bad (or at least, that we're not as bad as the next person). Have you ever tried to confess sin to God and not been able to come up with anything much? I have, and it wasn't because I hadn't sinned that day—it's because I'm blind to so much of it. This passage makes it clear that we do sin. It's not just that we put on a front to others to look good; we even lie to ourselves about how much, or how often, or how badly, or how deliberately we mess things up.

And even worse, when we cover up sin—making out as if it isn't a problem for us—we instead make out that God is the one who is being deceitful: "If we claim we have not sinned, we make [God] out to be a liar and his word is not in us" (v 9). Most of us would never say outright, "God is a liar." But we know from elsewhere in the Bible that God says all have sinned and all fall short of his glorious standards (Romans 3 v 23). So to deny that I sin is to say that he's wrong, and that while others may sin, I'm the exception.

Living like this is exhausting. My deception requires that I continue desperately working to prove my sinlessness and to cover up my failures. But living like this is a fraught existence. Can I ever have true peace? Will my efforts ever be enough? Of course not. I'll always be restless and weary, trying to justify myself.

And notice the implication of John's statement here: if we say we haven't sinned, not only do we make God out to be a liar but "his word is not in us" (v 10). We will never experience the peace of his forgiveness if we deny the truth of his word—that we are sinners in need of a Savior. We can't receive forgiveness if we don't think we need it.

I recently watched an old episode of a TV show from the early 90s in which a teenage girl got her first large pimple. She spent the whole episode worrying about it, applying cover-up, and placing her hands over her face strategically to hide it from others. None of these efforts actually got rid of the zit, but she expended a lot of energy trying to control it, and along with that people's perception of her. This is a somewhat gross image of what it's like when we try to cover our sin. We spend all our time and energy focusing on hiding what we can't take away. It's exhausting.

Every one of us is a sinner. And even if you've known this since you were in Sunday school, it's still worth remembering. It's sobering and humbling to remember that our natural inclination is not to admit our sin but to cover it up—it's only by the work of God's Spirit in our hearts that we're able to truly see our sin and take "option 2".

## #2 'FESS UP

We've seen that covering up leads to fake friendships. But as counter-intuitive as it might seem, the way for you to truly connect with others… is to confess your sin before God.

John tells us what happens when we do this. First, we're totally cleansed from all sin and unrighteousness (v 7, v 9; notice that John considers this important enough to mention twice). We're able to be made spotlessly clean, because we have "an advocate with the Father—Jesus Christ, the Righteous One" (2 v 1). God does not ask us to clean ourselves up and then come into the light so we can have fellowship with him. When we come into the light, covered in sin and shame, he has already provided what we need to be cleansed—his Son's blood. So however guilty we feel, and however much we fear exposure, when we step into the light and confess our sins, we have this promise: "He is faithful and just and will forgive us our sins and purify us from all unrighteousness" (1 v 9).

You might think, "Well, I already did that when I became a Christian. Jesus already cleansed me." And this is true. If you've trusted Jesus Christ for salvation from the penalty of sin, you have been cleansed. But John's audience here is Christians (see how he calls them "dear children" in 2 v 1)—those who have been forgiven and cleansed already. Yet he still instructs them to confess their sins, and assures them of forgiveness when they do, "so that [they] will not sin" (2 v 1). A regular pattern of repentance helps us to fight sin; it reminds us of how much Christ loves us and what it cost him to cleanse us, and drives us to live in a way that honors him. It reminds us that we're not lost causes; a clean slate motivates us to clean living.

So John is calling you to regular confession and repentance, born out of a love for God and a desire to not continue to sin.

But don't miss the detail in 1 v 7: it's when we're purified "from all sin" that we have "fellowship with one another." This is the surprising secret to deeper relationships: confessing our sin before God.

Why? Because the one anothers of verse 7 are in the same boat as we are—they need "the blood of Jesus" too. Church should not be a place where people cover their sin, but a community of forgiven sinners walking in the light together. When I'm honest with myself and with God, I'm reminded of his complete and total forgiveness, and this frees me to be vulnerable with others. After all, if you and I both know we need God's forgiveness, and we both know we have God's forgiveness, what is there left to hide from each other?

So when we're assured of our Father's forgiveness, instead of covering up in front of others, we can "confess"—be honest about our sin. If I look around church and compare myself to everyone's public "cover-up" faces, I will either be crushed by the comparison or redouble my efforts at pretending as they do. But when I look to Christ and am assured of God's forgiveness, neither of these will happen—I'm able to be honest about my weaknesses and vulnerable about my sin, and enjoy the deep relationships I long for because I'm not hiding or faking.

Are you a coverer or a confessor? I'll admit that for most of my life I never gave this question any thought. I pride myself on being independent, and not emotional or needy. But, as we'll see as we go along, this is not who God created me to be. Dependence is not weakness. Vulnerability is strength. And before God, any attempt to cover my own sin is futile and arrogant. He has already cleansed me of my sin—how pointless is it for me to try to cover it on my own?

Who is it that you're living a lie for? Here's what this "coverer tendency" looks like for me. I'm an "I'm fine" kind of girl. An older friend recently called me out on this. She said, "You're the person who always says 'I'm fine' when I ask you how things are going." I'm constantly struggling against the temptation to present a front of perfection. But I'm learning instead to embrace the beauty of the body of Christ. I'm learning that my ability to admit my struggles and sin is actually a way to build up my sisters and brothers in Christ. When I cover my sin, I cause others to feel alone—as if there's something wrong with them. But when I'm open and honest, I help create a safe space for others to do likewise.

I'm also learning how this tendency to hide my sin affects my children. My husband and I were talking with our kids about certain sin issues we saw in them, and we said, "We know what this is like because we sin too." Their response shocked us. "You don't ever sin," they said. Now trust me, this is ridiculous. They see my sin more than anyone else! But because we don't talk to them about it enough and don't identify it as "sin," they have easily believed that we don't struggle with disobeying God like they do. The natural outcome of this is a harmful belief that there's something wrong and different about them—they aren't "good" like their parents.

But when I intentionally bring my sin into the light, this act of confession creates a bond—a fellowship—with my children. In our home we talk a lot about being on the "same team." Rather than parents v kids, we are trying to create an atmosphere where all of us are together, fighting side by side against our sin and self-ishness. When I confess my sin to God in front of my kids, I show them they aren't alone. We're all in this to-gether, and God's grace is sufficient to cover it all. And isn't this the same atmosphere we long to experience in the church? Rather than opponents or rivals, we should view ourselves as a team which is struggling side by side against our sin—and that means we must be honest with our teammates.

As we go forward in this book, we will look at why we struggle with sin, how to confess, how to identify our sins at the root level, and specifically how to fight our sin together. But before we get there, I want you to know that I am living proof that the pain and discomfort of vulnerability is worth it. None of this is natural or easy for me, but it has changed my life.

If you are reading this book in a group, invite your fellow group-members to commit to working at vulnerability together. And if you're reading alone, maybe find a friend who will read and grow along with you. It's worth saying that it's wise to only cultivate close, confidential, one-to-one friendships with people of the same sex as you. That's not to say that brothers and sisters cannot be friends, or encourage and challenge one another—far from it. But single-sex Christian friendships for accountability guard against dangers that we should not be naive about (1 Timothy 5 v 1-2).

The joy on the other side of this kind of honesty is well worth the awkward beginning. We were not made for a finsta/rinsta world. We aren't meant to live in darkness and shame, hiding because we're afraid that if anyone really knew what our hearts are like, they wouldn't want anything to do with us.

And wonderfully, because the blood of Jesus "purifies us from all sin" (v 7), and because Jesus is our "advocate with the Father" (2 v 1), we can be assured that true fellowship with God and others is possible. We can walk in the light, experiencing the joy of true fellowship with our Father and his Son, our Savior. We can enjoy the kind of linked-arms community only possible among saved sinners walking the same path. In Christ we get the privilege of not only being witnesses of each other's lives, but also fellow laborers and brothers and sisters.

So let's learn to confess and battle our sin together—because true peace and deep relationships are possible through honesty about our struggles and our need for a Savior.

## REFLECT

- Do you let friends know the "real" you? What barriers keep you from opening up and being honest?
- Is it easier for you to be transparent with people in "real" life, or online? Why?
- Do you tend to be a "coverer" or a "confessor" (or both)? How do you see this play out in your day-to-day life?
- What are you hoping you'll gain from reading this book? Are you hoping for deeper, more transparent relationships? Take a minute and pray for God to work in and around you as you read this book.

# 2. THE WAY WE WERE

*I* am an uncrushable optimist when it comes to hours in a day. I constantly overestimate the amount of time I have, while underestimating how long it will take to do the things I need to do.

This is not one of my more endearing qualities because inevitably it means I will be late. For everything. I think I can sleep a little longer and still be ready on time. I think I can shower and dry my hair in 10 minutes, so I drink an extra cup of coffee first. Driving hurriedly to my destination, I come up with reasons for why I'm late. If I hit traffic on the interstate or get behind a slow driver, I'm thankful for the excuse, even though I would have been late on my own. *Road work? Yes! Rubber necking? Hurray! My kid threw a fit? Not my fault!*

For years this has been a matter of strife in my marriage. Generally, my husband is a patient, non-confrontational, forbearing man. But Sunday after Sunday, as he and the kids wait in the car for me to get ready for church, his blood pressure rises. I get in, tell him what went wrong this week that made me unexpectedly late, and apologize. He says, "It's okay," and then just sits there, silently. And I can't handle *that*—either reassure me that it's no big deal, or accuse me so I can defend myself. Don't just stay quiet.

So I sit. And think. And eventually the Spirit brings me to the point of seeing the root of it all—my selfishness and pride. I'm selfish in thinking my time and my desires are more important than those of my family. And I'm prideful in thinking I can do everything and still be on time. So I ask Erik to forgive me, which he does.

And then the following Sunday we start the process all over again.

Flash forward to one Sunday in the recent past. Amazingly, I was ready. The kids were ready. And guess who wasn't? That's right. And I just can't tell you the satisfaction I felt when I made a big deal about saying, "Okay, kids, come get in the car. We'll wait for Dad out there." As I sat there when he got in, my self-righteousness was bubbling over. I was mad that we were late, but I was just so glad he could see what it's really like to rush around, feeling guilty about making the family late. But when he asked me to forgive him, I was immediately convicted about my pride and my weird desire to make my husband feel bad.

My Sunday-morning lateness is just one seemingly small area where I feel guilt, and even shame, about ongoing sin. Shouldn't I have mastered this one by now? There are practical steps I can take to be on time. But the issue is deeper, and in this and many areas, I can eventually beat myself up about the ongoing struggle to the point that I just want to give up completely.

## WHY THIS MATTERS

We all have things we try to overcome—tendencies to sin in certain areas. It could be gossip, materialism, lust, the outworking of anger, a lack of self-control (with spending, eating, drinking, TV-watching, overworking, and so on). These sins cause us to feel guilt, and the guilt over time leads to shame, both imposed by ourselves and others. We wonder why God doesn't give us mastery over our sin. I promise myself every Sunday that the next week will be different. Or every time I find myself envying a friend's life and begrudging what she has, I tell myself I mustn't do that again.

Perhaps the answer to our guilt is to cut ourselves some slack and decide that it's not that big a deal. It's common for people to say things like, "Give yourself grace." But what does that mean? Is it okay to just excuse some of these things? After all, they could be worse.

Maybe so—but to brush our sin aside as insignificant is to live in denial. As we saw in the last chapter, hiding or denying our sin helps no one, least of all ourselves. We can't ignore the fact that our sin—whether we view it as big or small, shame-inducing or shruggable—can deeply affect our relationships with the people we love most. Every day we experience the pain of strained relationships to one degree or another.

So why are things so hard? Where does this tension in our relationships come from? Why does sin plague us the way it does?

That's what we'll think about in this chapter. For many of us, this is familiar ground, and we're tempted to skate over it. But if we struggle in any way with sin or deceit or covering up (yep, that's all of us), then even if it's for the hundredth time, we need to read it again.

## WHAT WE WERE MADE FOR

There was a time when relationships weren't hard. This cycle of shame and guilt and strain isn't what we were made for. Back in Genesis chapters 1 and 2, God designed a perfect world, and then made humans in his image to live in harmony and work together to rule over his creation:

> *Then God said, "Let us make mankind in our image, in our likeness, so that they may rule over the fish in the sea and the birds in the sky, over the livestock and all the wild animals, and over all the creatures that move along the ground."*
>
> *So God created mankind in his own image, in the image of God he created them; male and female he created them.*
>
> *(Genesis 1 v 26-27)*

This verse comes after a long description of how God created our world in all its dazzling diversity. But up to this point, never is this phrase—"in our image"— used. The earth is not made in God's image. The birds are not made in God's image. The beasts are not made in God's image. But man and woman are. This truth is what theologians call the *imago dei*— we are made in the image of God.

Our Creator looked at all he had made, and about every part of it he said, *It is good.* But with man and woman on the scene, creation became "very good" (1 v 31). In making us in his image, he gave us abilities and responsibilities, purpose and identity. Which means that our status as image-bearers has profound implications for how we are meant to live.

First, being made in God's image has implications for how we relate to him. We are made to live in dependence upon him. The 5th-century bishop and theologian Augustine wrote, "You have made us for yourself, and our heart is restless until it rests in you" (*Confessions*, p 3). Put simply, we need him. And what could be better than dependence on the loving Creator who formed us—who made us to be like him, and to know him? We read that God walked in the Garden of Eden with the first man and woman—this was not the relationship of a power-monger with a minion. This was a loving Father, faithfully orchestrating the best for his children.

Second, the *imago dei* has implications for the way we relate with other image-bearers. As we saw in the last chapter, just as the members of the Trinity live in fellowship and unity, our being made in the image of the Trinity means we too are made for that kind of fellowship. Our *imago-dei* reality means we were designed for perfect relationships with others. We see this in the beautiful way in which Adam and Eve related to one another: they "were both naked, and they felt no shame" (2 v 25). They had no shame-induced desire to cover themselves. They were living in perfect harmony.

Third, our identity as image-bearers has implications for our relationship with creation. "Image-bearer" is a title that comes with a job description:

> *God blessed them and said to them, "Be fruitful and increase in number; fill the earth and subdue it. Rule over the fish in the sea and the birds in the sky and over every living creature that moves on the ground."*
> *(Genesis 1 v 28)*

Before Adam and Eve ever sinned, God gave his image-bearers the gift of work. As stewards over creation, we reflect something of our Creator. This means that as we work as teachers, lawyers, homemakers, grandmothers, software developers, artists, nurses, and whatever else we do, we are told to seek the good of creation.

This is how it was meant to be: God's image-bearers living in communion with him, with each other, and with the world he created. Life was truly good.

And then it all fell apart.

## RELATIONSHIPS UNRAVELED

It's hard to read Genesis chapters 1 and 2 and not lament what comes next in the account of Adam and Eve. Having been given everything they could possibly want, they chose to disobey God.

He told them there was one tree—one tree out of so *many*—from which they could not eat. And he even told them why, saying, "But you must not eat from the tree of the knowledge of good and evil, for when you eat from it you will certainly die" (2 v 17).

Yet Genesis 3 shows us that they did just what he told them not to.

There have been many times when I've read this part of the Bible and wanted to shake Adam and Eve by the shoulders and yell, "You guys are so stupid. You had one rule! I'm sure I could have kept it."

But it's not quite as simple as that—because into the story slithers a serpent. And the first thing he does is to twist God's words to cause Eve to doubt. He says, "Did God really say, 'You must not eat from any tree in the garden'?" (3 v 1) Eve answers that they may eat of the trees in the garden, but just not the one "in the middle of the garden" (v 3).

As a child, my brother and I weren't allowed to watch the same TV shows and movies as my cousins. Of course, this meant that when we were together, we were the cause of exasperation to cousins who wanted to watch the latest blockbusters to come out on VHS, and instead were stuck watching *Annie* for the 30th time. They complained that our parents wouldn't let us watch anything. Hearing this, I started to agree. "Yeah, why won't you guys let us watch anything? Everyone else can do it. It's fine. You just don't want us to have fun." Never mind that there were hundreds of things we *could* watch. Suddenly, I was fixated on what I couldn't have.

This is a bit like what happens between Eve and the serpent. What formerly seemed like abundance and plenty now feels like restriction. She tells him that God said if they eat the fruit of the tree or touch it, they will die. But the serpent says, "You will not certainly die. For God knows that when you eat from it your eyes will be opened, and you will be like God, knowing good and evil" (v 4). In an instant, he dismantles everything God has shown Adam and Eve about himself. The serpent calls God a liar and tells Eve that he is withholding something good that she is entitled to. A loving God would not do that. So Eve is faced with two possibilities: either God is loving and the serpent is lying, or God is lying and the serpent is kindly looking out for the humans' best interests.

We read Genesis 3 with the benefit of knowing who the serpent was—Satan, the great deceiver, the enemy of God (Revelation 12 v 9). But Eve hears his words and decides that it is God who is lying—instantly what she knows of her Creator is cast aside. "When the woman saw that the fruit of the tree was good for food and pleasing to the eye, and also desirable for gaining wisdom, she took some and ate it. She also gave some to her husband, who was with her, and he ate it" (Genesis 3 v 6). It's as if the serpent's words cause her to truly look at the tree for the first time. She sees that the food looks good; it's a delight, and it promises her something desirable. She doesn't resist the urge to take and eat.

And everything comes crashing down around her. In a meditation on Psalm 78, Tim and Kathy Keller write, "God created the world, so when we disobey him we unleash forces of chaos and disorder. When you, a being created to live for God, live instead for yourself, you violate your design" (*The Songs of Jesus*, p 189). This is what we see happen in the post-sin reality of Genesis 3.

All three aspects of the *imago dei*—relationship with God, relationship with other image-bearers, and relationship with creation—are changed in an instant as the first man and woman eat the forbidden fruit. Their communion with God is broken—they go from walking with God to running and hiding from him.

When God finds them and asks them what happened, Adam blames Eve, while Eve in turn blames the serpent. If you've spent much time with children, you've no doubt seen this scene play out. We're natural hiders. Shame does this. It makes us run: we make excuses and hope somehow we can take it all back.

And it gets worse, as Adam tells God, "The woman *you put here with me*—she gave me some fruit from the tree, and I ate it" (3 v 12, emphasis mine). Adam is not just blaming Eve—he's ultimately blaming God.

And their relationship with each other is broken too. For the first time, they are ashamed of their nakedness and they want to hide their bodies. Having chosen their own path instead of God's good design, their desire is not just to cover up in front of God, but also one another.

And instead of caring for creation, from now on they'll be in a state of war with the thorns and thistles the ground produces, battling the elements to keep themselves alive (v 17-19).

Everything was so good—and now it's all wrecked.

## SEEING THE CYCLE

Genesis 3 is a spiritual and relational car crash—but we're not just standing by as witnesses to the horror. We're in the car too.

This is the cycle we experience when we sin. We believe the lie that living for God is too restrictive. He doesn't really have our best interests at heart. We want to do things our own way. We want to take control. And when we do, our sin brings shame, blame, and discord. It wreaks havoc on our relationships.

I'm guessing that right now, there's something you want. It might be something good—marriage, a child, a new job, a home, a raise, a friend. Imagine that you ask God for this thing over and over again. You wait expectantly, but as the days and months and even years go by, it still hasn't happened. You start to doubt God's goodness. Why would he withhold this thing from you? You hide from him, bitter and ashamed of your doubt.

Your horizontal relationships, too, are affected. Your friend just got a new job and you can't be excited for her. Your sister and her husband just bought a new home, and you can't bear to be around their happiness. Your Instagram feed is full of women having girls' nights and taking selfies with their best friends, so you start to cut people off because they have what you don't.

In one sense you've not "*done*" anything—it's not like you ate forbidden fruit. You just questioned why you can't have this good thing.

But this is the attitude that chokes us. This is what sin does. It slithers around in us, causing us to believe lies about God. It places our own visions of happiness above all else, telling us to do what it takes to get what we want or to cut off those who won't let us have it. And the shame of it all causes us to withdraw and hide. We feel burdened by it. *No one else would understand,* we think. *It's been too much, too long—God can't possibly take me back. My friends don't want to hear this.*

Sometimes, though, it's not about some big thing we want. Much more often, our sin stems from far simpler things. For instance, the other day I was trying to get my kids out of the house to go pick up breakfast at Chick-fil-A. It was "Cow Appreciation Day," when dressing like a cow earns you a free entrée. But one of my children was not thrilled about having to wear spots on his or her shirt. And the other child was talking incessantly. And my husband was working from home. And my temper rose rapidly. The next thing I know, I'm lecturing both kids (loudly enough for their father to hear) about how "Dad's working from home so we have to be quiet, and that's why I'm trying to get you out of the house. I'm just trying to do something nice for you all."

In that moment, even as the words were coming out of my mouth, I knew how wrong I was. First, my husband never asked us to be quiet. He never asked us to leave. Second, it's understandable to not want to dress as a cow. For a maturing child, that can be socially humiliating. The truth is that I was the one who wanted to go get free breakfast, not because we needed to get out but because those chicken biscuits are one of the greatest things America has ever produced.

But see what happened in that moment? I noticed myself losing control, and my pride wouldn't let me admit it. *Yeah, maybe I'm getting a little intense, but obviously it's because I'm just trying to help everyone.* And the implication was that it was my husband's fault. If he wasn't working from home, we wouldn't have to leave. And if we didn't have to leave, I wouldn't be so angry right now.

The truth is that at the bottom of it all, I crave a life of ease and freedom. I want to go where I want, spend what I want, do what I want. And when someone steps in the way or makes me wait, I easily lose control. Rather than enjoying some extra time with my husband or comforting my concerned child, I pushed through to go where I wanted to go, with casualties in tow.

What about you? Your struggles may look different, but everyone has them. Think back to the last time you spoke out in anger, or simmered in bitter resentment about another person or situation. Try to go deeper and see what deep-seated desires were driving your decisions and relationships in that moment. Maybe it was a desire for control, or a hunger to be respected and valued.

Or how do you see yourself blaming others when things don't go your way? Who do you tend to blame? Your roommate who kept you up last night? Your parents who brought you up wrongly? Your boss who is setting the deadlines? Underneath it all, perhaps you blame God himself, who gave you your roommate/parents/boss.

Adam's and Eve's responses in the garden—their embarrassing displays of finger-pointing and blame-shifting—are painful examples of what we all do. Having believed a lie, we reject God, and now our relationships suffer the consequences. It's sin that makes friendships painful—and sin that makes them shallow.

## THE HERO WHO CAN

Adam and Eve traded in their greatest treasure for a tree—they were willing to give up fellowship with God for a piece of fruit.

In his righteous anger over their sin, God laid out the way the world would change because of their choice. Childbirth would be painful, the relationship between men and women would be strained, the ground would be cursed and hard to work, and ultimately, they would die. Instead of living forever in paradise, they were removed from the garden to labor and toil and live out their lives until death (3 v 16-19). God sent them from the garden to protect them from an eternity of living in their current condition. Living forever in sin and shame was not paradise as it was intended.

We, too, face God's righteous anger for our sin. Only instead of being removed from paradise, we face eternity in hell. God's desire was to dwell with his image-bearers, but by rejecting him we submitted to eternal separation from the One who made us and loves us dearly.

But God gave them, and gives us, hope. God promised that one day, a descendant of the woman would "crush" the serpent's head (Genesis 3 v 14-15). Then, in another act of mercy, we read that "the Lord God made garments of skin for Adam and his wife and clothed them" (3 v 21). This is the first animal sacrifice: an animal was put to death to cover the sins of God's image-bearers. Just as we do now, Adam and Eve had tried to cover up their own shame, quickly cobbling together fig leaves to hide their nakedness. But it's only God's actions that can deal with their shame and enable the man and woman to look one another in the eye again. It was all a picture of what the promised offspring of the woman—Jesus Christ—would one day do for the world. Much more than covering our outward shame, his death cleanses us from inward sin and shame.

In the 2017 film *Wonder Woman*, actress Gal Gadot portrays the female superhero as an outsider coming from an island paradise to rescue mankind at war. But she is not one of us. She is a deity—part Amazonian and part Greek goddess—and she stands in judgment on humanity and our lack of love and kindness toward one another. Rather than being cold and aloof, she chooses to love mankind and to serve the world with her protection. But she makes an interesting statement at the end of the film:

> *I used to want to save the world. To end war and bring peace to mankind. But then I glimpsed the darkness that lives within their light. And I learned that inside every one of them, there will always be both—a choice each must make for themselves. Something no hero will ever defeat. And now I know that only love can truly save the world. So I stay, I fight, and I give, for the world I know can be.*

She's right that there is a lot of darkness in the world. And love *is* the only thing that can save us. But while Wonder Woman is not the heroine who can save us from this darkness, there is someone who can. What we need is not a hero who retains their powers and stands apart from us. We need a hero who gave up all his privileges to truly become one of us—not a god-dressed-as-human but God-made-flesh. Our hope is in the One who made us in his image, and then took on our image to rescue us from ourselves. It's his love alone that can save us.

We're not done with thinking about our sin and our struggles yet—in the next few chapters we'll dig a little deeper into the darkness in our own hearts. This will not be comfortable. But as we learn to identify our sins and repent of them—and as we open up with others to share our struggles—we will not be overcome by them. We can rejoice in the One who fulfilled the prophecy of Genesis 3, crushing the serpent's head and defeating sin and death for his image-bearers. If you have trusted in Christ's saving work on the cross and in his resurrection power, then your identity is not just a bearer of God's image, but also God's child. We can rest in that identity, even as we fight against our sin.

In Christ, our relationship with God is already restored—and as we'll see, he is also in the business of restoring our relationships with others.

### REFLECT

- What sins do you feel that you just keep struggling with?
- Can you identify any lies you've been believing about God? For example, "God must not love me because…"
- Adam and Eve played the blame game after they disobeyed God in Eden. Is there anyone you tend to blame for your sin? Why do you think that is?
- Isn't it a comfort to know that Jesus' death doesn't just cleanse our outward shame, but also the guilt and shame inside us? As we become more aware of our sin, it makes us more amazed at his grace. Spend some time praising him now.

# 3. TRUE TO YOURSELF?

The story of David and Bathsheba is one of those stories that children's-ministry leaders dread. How do you teach the gravity of adultery and murder without, you know, talking to a four-year-old about adultery and murder?

Yet this episode is key in understanding both the consequences and effects of sin, as well as the immense grace and forgiveness of God. In this chapter, we will dig into the story. Then in the next chapter, we'll meditate our way through the prayer of repentance that David wrote in response—Psalm 51—and use it as a pattern for our own confession. The narrative is not pretty, but it's one of the stories that gives me great hope that God loves sinners.

In the years leading up to this moment, David had gone from lowly shepherd boy to king of Israel; from protector of sheep to military hero. In 2 Samuel 10 we see Israel battling the Arameans and Ammonites. The Ammonites had offended David and the nation of Israel, and in fear of Israel they hired the Arameans to fight with them. But when David and his men defeated the Arameans, the Ammonites were left to fight on their own.

So this brings us to 2 Samuel 11 v 1:

> *In the spring, at the time when kings go off to war,*
> *David sent Joab out with the king's men and the whole*
> *Israelite army. They destroyed the Ammonites and*
> *besieged Rabbah. But David remained in Jerusalem.*

This first verse tips us off that something is not quite right. It's the time when kings go off to war, and this time David, who had previously fought alongside his men, stays home when the army goes out. So what does he do instead? Verse 2 says:

> *One evening David got up from his bed and walked*
> *around on the roof of the palace. From the roof he*
> *saw a woman bathing. The woman was very beautiful.*

David finds out who the woman is (Bathsheba), and to whom she's married (Uriah). Yet he proceeds to send messengers to bring her to him, and sleeps with her (some scholars use the term "rape" because the text implies she had no choice but to comply). She then returns home and eventually sends word to David that she has conceived his child.

Panic sets in, and David develops what might have been a decent cover-up plan were it not for the integrity of Bathsheba's husband. David brings her husband, Uriah, home from the battlefront. He encourages Uriah to go to his house in hopes he will go to bed with his wife and so think that the baby is his, but Uriah will not go, choosing instead to be loyal to the king while the rest of his brothers are on the battlefield. Apparently, David did not expect Uriah to be able to control his desires. After all, David did not control *his*.

When his plan fails, David can see no option other than having Uriah killed to cover his own sin. To ensure Uriah's death, he instructs his military commander, Joab, to place Uriah in the front of the hardest fighting, and then draw back and leave him there.

A messenger comes to the king and tells him the plan has been carried out. David sends a message back to Joab: "The sword devours one as well as another" (2 Samuel 11 v 25). In other words, *These things happen. Don't worry about it.* Uriah is an unfortunate casualty resulting from David's selfishness. As he is king, it looks as if he can do as he pleases with no consequences. So after the mourning period he takes Bathsheba as his wife, and she gives birth to a son.

David's got what he wanted and we can assume that he's happy. For nine months or more, it seems that he's gotten away with it. Yet we read these words in verse 27:

*But the thing David had done displeased the LORD.*

This verse strikes an ominous tone. It's like reading Shakespeare's *Macbeth*, in which Macbeth and his wife go about making him king through murder. They achieve what they desire, but the tone of the play clues you in to the fact that it's not going to end well for either of them.

At the end of 2 Samuel 11, we know God is going to act. He is not fooled by David's charade of domestic bliss. He knows, he sees, and he's displeased. He won't just sit by and let his servant get away with sin.

## A SEVERE MERCY

Cue stage right—the prophet Nathan, who enters with all the flourish of a Shakespearean storyteller. He tells David a story about two men: a rich man with many herds and flocks, and a poor man with only one little ewe lamb. The poor man treats the lamb like a member of his family—it grows up with his children, eats from his table, and sleeps in his bed. Nathan says this lamb "was like a daughter to" the poor man (2 Samuel 12 v 3). If you've ever had a beloved pet, you can probably relate.

Then a traveler comes to visit the rich man. The rich man needs an animal to feed his guest, but rather than taking one from his large flocks and herds, he takes the poor man's lamb and feeds it to the traveler.

David sees the obvious injustice here, angrily saying, "As surely as the Lord lives, the man who did this must die! He must pay for that lamb four times over, because he did such a thing and had no pity" (12 v 5-6). But the tables are turned as Nathan delivers his dramatic next line:

*You are the man!*

Instead of another man's lamb, David has taken something much more precious—another man's wife. And just as the rich man had plenty of lambs of his own, David already has more than one wife. He was not in need. Through Nathan the Lord rebukes David, recounting all the things he has given him, and saying that if this weren't enough, he would have given him "even more." But David grasped for more with his own grubby hands; he has despised "the word of the LORD by doing what is evil in his eyes" (v 9). And now he will suffer the consequences of his actions for years to come:

> *Now, therefore, the sword will never depart from your house, because you despised me and took the wife of Uriah the Hittite to be your own.*
>
> *This is what the LORD says: "Out of your own household I am going to bring calamity on you. Before your very eyes I will take your wives and give them to one who is close to you, and he will sleep with your wives in broad daylight. You did it in secret, but I will do this thing in broad daylight before all Israel."*
>
> *(12 v 10-12)*

Those verses can feel shocking and distasteful, and that's because they are. We get a glimpse here of how serious sin is. Through the rest of David's life, we see these consequences play out. First, the baby conceived with Bathsheba dies. Then David's son Amnon rapes his half-sister, Tamar, and is murdered by her brother Absalom. In a sickening fulfillment of Nathan's prophecy, Absalom goes on to betray his father and take over the palace, where he sleeps with David's concubines "in the sight of all Israel" (2 Samuel 16 v 22).

David's sin has long-lasting consequences. Yet, at the moment when Nathan speaks God's word to him, David is not concerned about the consequences; he's struck by his sin. His first response is, "I have sinned against the LORD" (12 v 13). This is a turn of phrase implying true repentance—it's an opening of the eyes to the true condition of the heart. God has intervened to show him the true poisonous horror of his actions.

## SUBTLE STORIES

This narrative is pretty straightforward: David sees something he wants, and then sinfully takes it. But our culture has a way of telling similar stories that is much more subtle. We tend to praise ideas like "being true to myself" or "living my truth." Recently, my Facebook feed has been full of stories about women ending their marriages to pursue their true identities, leading to what they regard as greater independence and freedom. Underneath these so-called "vulnerable" posts, we find comment after comment heralding these women for their bravery in pursuing true happiness.

I certainly don't want to be insensitive to the struggles of living in a difficult marriage. These women may have experienced things that have crushed them and made them feel they have little value. This is devastatingly true in far too many marriages. And to be clear: it is right to remove oneself from an abusive marriage.

What I'm talking about here is something different: the increasing glorification in our culture of what we want—"our truth"—as what is right. *It must be right, because I want it.* Yet when we pursue "our truth," there will always be casualties. Often we chase after our own happiness at the expense of those around us—children, family members, friends. What the world deems to be "good"—being true to our own desires—can leave a wide wake of sorrow behind us.

And whether or not we act on them, our desires themselves usually reveal an ugly heart. When my mind wanders to what I'd rather be doing, my thoughts are often self-absorbed and self-exalting. At this moment in time, following my impulse for happiness would mean driving seven hours to the beach by myself for a long weekend of solitude. Or driving across town to a favorite clothing store to spend far too much money. In some moments, my desires might be a bit more loving—the desire to spend time and money on a friend or a family member, for instance. But for the most part, my immediate thoughts are not about how my choices will affect those around me; much like David, my decisions can leave a wake of pain for other people.

What about you? Where does your mind wander when you're driving someplace on your own? What are the scenes that you play out in your head when you're in the shower or cooking dinner? Deep down, are your heart's desires at times self-absorbed and self-exalting?

I'm guessing the answer to that last question is "yes." This is why the Bible says our hearts are deceitful and wicked (Jeremiah 17 v 9). Apart from the Spirit's work in our lives, our desires are motivated by our own selfishness. We see this from Genesis 3 on.

Another way the Bible talks about this is in terms of "idolatry." In the Old Testament, God's people were surrounded by nations who worshiped manmade gods, or idols, and time and again they were pulled into doing the same thing—worshiping created things rather than their Creator.

Our idols today may not be statues, but we still have things that compete with God for our worship—things that we hold as more precious than him. Often we make an idol out of what we think we want and need—pursuing it, prizing it, possessing it—rather than worshiping the God who gives us everything we truly need. We chase happiness at the expense of those around us, and at the expense of our relationship with our Creator—the One who can make us truly joyful.

## WHAT SIN COSTS

One of my favorite books to read to my children is *My Lucky Day* by Keiko Kasza. It's the story of a wolf who finds a pig on his doorstep and thinks his dinner has just delivered itself to his door. What he does not know is that the pig has a master plan, and by the end of the story, the wolf, thinking he was preparing the pig to consume, has given him a bath, fed him a huge meal, and massaged him. Eventually the wolf falls asleep from exhaustion, and the pig skips home with a plate of leftover cookies, plotting his next escapade at the bear's house.

The wolf loses his ability to think clearly and see through the pig's ploys because he's so distracted by his own desires. He falls prey because of his appetite.

The same can be said of David. Having already made the choice to remain at home, rather than fulfilling his duties as a king, he sees something he wants and takes it, apparently giving no thought to how his choice might affect others. And the effects of his choices are devastating to many.

First, he betrays his men. He should be with them, but instead he's at home, comfortable in his palace. It's hard to trust a leader who abandons his duties in his own pursuit of comfort.

Second, he uses Bathsheba, with no thought of her own marriage. The Bible doesn't spell out whether Bathsheba desires this adulterous act with the king. We do know, however, that David is a man in a position of power, using that power to get what he wants. He sacrifices Bathsheba's reputation and marriage for his own momentary pleasure.

Third—and most obviously—he wrongs Uriah: first by sleeping with his wife, and then with his cover-up plan. He attempts to sacrifice Uriah's integrity as a soldier by tempting him to compromise and sleep with his wife, even though such an act was forbidden for a military man during times of war. When he cannot convince Uriah to do this, he arranges to have him killed.

We also see the way it affects David's commander, Joab, who is forced to send Uriah to his death in an act he surely knows is suspicious. And what about David's other servants? Who else knew about David's actions and was obliged to keep quiet for him? Many of us have worked for people we don't respect. How quickly this leads to bitterness and dissatisfaction.

Finally, David's sin meant the death of his child. 2 Samuel 12 v 15-18 says:

> *The LORD struck the child that Uriah's wife had borne to David, and he became ill. David pleaded with God for the child. He fasted and spent the nights lying in sackcloth on the ground. The elders of his household stood beside him to get him up from the ground, but he refused, and he would not eat any food with them. On the seventh day the child died.*

David pursued what he believed would make him happy. While David may have been sitting pretty and feeling good until Nathan arrived, his actions wreaked havoc on all those around him.

And, as Adam and Eve discovered, pursuing happiness apart from God doesn't work for long. David has forgotten the joy of walking with God—he's consumed by his own appetites, he spurns the good gifts he already has from a good God, and he goes after something else (v 8-9). He's so fixated on what he wants that he either doesn't see or doesn't care about the consequences for others.

Our sin does not just affect us—it affects those around us. Some, like Bathsheba and Uriah, are directly affected in deep and personal ways. Others, like the soldiers and servants, are affected more indirectly. But sin—all sin, your sin—always costs someone, somehow.

But I suspect you already knew that. After all, can any of us say that we haven't ever hurt another person in the pursuit of our own desires? Or drawn another person into gossip, or made a cheap joke at their expense, just to make ourselves feel better? Which of us hasn't seen that look in another person's eyes—that stunned, wounded look—which says, "I trusted you, but now I'm not sure that I can." Or who hasn't walked away from a situation thinking, "I can't believe I did that/said that"?

I have—and I suspect you have too.

But even as our sin can break down our relationships, our relationships can also enable us to fight against our sin. We see this in Nathan, the man sent by God to call David to repentance.

When I got married, my college roommate and volleyball teammate, Randi, gave my husband a strange wedding gift: a volleyball and a stack of Post-It notes. While he had no clue what to do with such a weird present, I immediately recognized the significance and laughed. In our second year as roommates, we went through a period where I was kind of a mess. We were experiencing a lot of conflict, and I was ignoring the wisdom and warnings of multiple caring friends. So one night, Randi locked the dorm room door to prevent interruptions, sat me down, and pulled out a volleyball covered with Post-It notes. On each she had written something she wanted to talk about with me—a mix of encouragement and confrontation.

Those who know me well know that this was a brave move! I've never met an argument I didn't rise to. So confronting me was not easy or comfortable for Randi. She could have just left me to my self-destruction— we could have gone on living alongside each other in a tense atmosphere, eventually ignoring one other as much as possible.

But Randi loved me enough to take the hard road. She risked alienation for my sake, and chose to point out my blind spots and lovingly call me to repentance. It was not an easy conversation, but it was a turning point for me.

We later laughed about the ball and the notes, and she gave them to my husband to pass on the torch. (Thankfully, he's never had to use them. Or maybe he's been too scared I would spike it in his face.)

Just as God used Nathan to show David his sin, Randi was a "Nathan" in my life in that moment. There have been others, including my husband, who have played this role at other times. Being a Nathan is no easy task. It must come from a place in your heart where you love the other person too much to watch him or her continue down a path you know will lead to destruction. There's no place for pride or bullying self-righteousness: "Brothers and sisters, if someone is caught in a sin, you who live by the Spirit should restore that person *gently*" (Galatians 6 v 1). Ignoring the sin to maintain the relationship will always feel like the easier option—but if you really love someone, you will be prepared to lose the relationship, at least for a time, if that's what it takes.

As well as being motivated by love, we must also be motivated by God's glory. Nathan was sent to David because the king had "despise[d] the word of the LORD" and was making a mockery of being God's chosen ruler (2 Samuel 12 v 9). There will be times when we look at a person's life and it's easy to doubt what the loving thing to do is, because they may seem genuinely happier as a result of the sinful decision they have made. But when God's glory and honor is our highest priority ("Love the Lord your God with all your heart ... soul ... strength and ... mind"), we will then be able to confront others in love ("Love your neighbor as yourself", see Luke 10 v 27). These are hard conversations—but when our motive is to see God honored, and to speak life and truth from his word into other people's lives, we will be willing to have them.

When we choose to be a Nathan, we won't always see a response like David's—sometimes that person won't listen. But we never know how things will work out later down the line: we read in 1 Chronicles 3 v 5 that David and Bathsheba named their third son Nathan, and this son is later mentioned in the genealogy of Christ (Luke 3 v 31). We can keep praying in hope for even the most distant, determined wanderers.

David's sin led to lasting consequences and so much heartache. This is a tale of warning, guiding us to resist trading it all away for a moment of pleasure. Our familiarity with this story might make us immune to the shock of David's soap-opera actions—but what should really leave us open-mouthed in surprise is 2 Samuel 12 v 13. David admits that he has "sinned against the LORD" and Nathan tells him, "The LORD has taken away your sin. You are not going to die."

Dereliction of duty, sexual assault, murder, lies—all that, just taken away? Don't let familiarity with the gospel rob you of the right reaction to Nathan's statement: *How? Why?*

In an episode of the British TV drama *Call the Midwife*, a woman dreads the birth of her baby because she knows her husband will then discover she has been unfaithful to him. Indeed, there is no overlooking the fact that the baby cannot be her husband's, as his skin color is not the same as the baby's. And yet, upon seeing the child for the first time, the husband's only remark is, "I don't reckon to know much about babies, but I can see how this is the most beautiful baby in the world." He is willfully ignorant of his wife's infidelity, refusing to condemn her and choosing instead to keep no record of her wrongdoing.

This is a beautiful story, and one that brought me to the point just shy of sobbing. But it falls short of the Bible's description of God's mercy to sinners. He cannot merely overlook our sin. If he did, he would no longer be just. A holy God cannot simply excuse the unholiness of sin. Instead, he must execute judgment upon sin, and he did so by pouring out his wrath for sin upon his Son in our place. This is how David's sin was taken away—not overlooked, but reserved to be put upon Another:

> *For all have sinned and fall short of the glory of God, and all are justified freely by his grace through the redemption that came by Christ Jesus. God presented Christ as a sacrifice of atonement, through the shedding of his blood—to be received by faith. He did this to demonstrate his righteousness, because in his forbearance he had left the sins committed beforehand unpunished—he did it to demonstrate his righteousness at the present time, so as to be just and the one who justifies those who have faith in Jesus.*
> *(Romans 3 v 23-26)*

In the same way, God is just in justifying us. He does not simply acquit us. The sin had to be punished, but the wrath was poured out on Christ. So then God declares us not only "not guilty," but also "righteous." The late Christian writer John Stott said "justification" is God's "righteous way of 'righteousing' the unrighteous" (*The Incomparable Christ*, p 53). It's not only "just as if I'd never sinned," but also "just as if I'd always obeyed." This is all of grace—God's astonishingly generous, liberating, free gift.

So if this chapter has made you conscious of how you've pursued your own desires at the expense of others—if you're left mourning the trail of broken hearts you've left in your wake—remember this grace.

Grace gives us forgiveness for even the worst of our sin, because the punishment we deserve has already been borne by Jesus.

Grace gives us fresh eyes and a hopeful expectation for our most broken relationships, because it means that restoration is always possible.

Grace motivates us to be Nathans to those in our lives, and to listen to the Nathans God has given us, because we know that God's truth is better than self-deceit.

When we're exposed to the emptiness of those things that can never truly satisfy us, it drives us instead to the only One who can—and as we run into his loving arms we will receive this grace. Again, and again, and again.

## REFLECT

- When David is confronted by Nathan and shown the consequences of his sin, what is his response? Is that your response when you're confronted about your sin? Why or why not?
- Why are the ideas of "following your heart" or "living your truth" so alluring? In what ways do they fail to live up to what they promise?
- Have you known any "Nathans" who have lovingly confronted you or someone else? How did they do it? How do we sometimes get this wrong?
- Why is it better that God justifies us, rather than merely acquitting us?

# 4. REHEARSING
# REPENTANCE

*I* was eight years old, sitting in the mauve-cushion-lined pews of our church building, nursing a runny nose with a tissue. At the close of the service as we stood to sing and walk out, I quickly stuffed the used tissue between the seat and the backrest, hoping no one would notice. Imagine my surprise when I returned home and was pulled aside by my father, who held the evidence of my laziness in his hands. He took the time to teach me about personal responsibility and thinking of others—in this case, the church janitor—more highly than myself. I accepted responsibility and expected that to be the end of it.

Yet in a stroke of parenting genius at which I now marvel, that was not the end of the matter. The following day I found myself, knees knocking, confessing my thoughtlessness to the church janitor himself, asking his forgiveness, and offering my services to him for the remainder of the day. It was terrifying.

Maybe you have a watershed confession story from your childhood. For my brother, it was the long, shameful walk up the street to ask the forgiveness of our neighbor Benjamin and his parents for a lassoing incident that my mom had watched in horror from the front window. My brother's defensive plea was that he never imagined he would *actually succeed* in getting the lasso around Benjamin's neck and pulling him off his bike. Yet there he was, asking for the forgiveness of our neighbors for the rope burn around their son's neck.

These incidents are funny now, although if you went through something similar as a kid, you'll understand that they seemed anything but funny at the time. You honestly do not think you will survive it. If you somehow manage to apologize without passing out or getting sick, you're sure you will never recover from the horror of it all. And, ironically, you're not sure you will ever forgive your parents for making you go through the experience. (I can now testify that not only do I forgive them, but I thank them for it. But it took a couple of decades.)

My relationship with repentance developed with the childhood ritual of asking my brother's forgiveness for a laundry list of vague sins from my bed at night. I would lie there after the lights were out, look across the hall to his own open door, and let my voice carry my contrition to his sleepy hearing. Having been warned not to let the sun go down on our anger, we made sure to cover all possibilities of sins we may have committed during the day. "Aaron, I'm sorry for yelling at you, hitting you, being selfish with the Nintendo, and tattling on you today. Will you forgive me?" His answer, along with his confession of the typical older-sibling sins counter to my own (pestering, bossing, manipulating) came back to my room in return. Thus we slept in the peace of the slightly remorseful.

Admittedly this is the narrative of children who grew up in a home where we were lovingly trained in the fear of the Lord. My parents were not perfect, but we knew we were loved. Because confession and repentance were fixtures in our home, I had a strong sense of right and wrong, and I felt the guilt of my own sins—even to the point of telling on myself frequently as I grew older. And yet in all this, my confessions were motivated more by fear of disappointing my parents or feeling guilty than fear of the Lord. I knew I was supposed to confess my sins to him, and I prayed many late-night fervent prayers in the hopes of securing my salvation after a particularly sin-filled day. Yet I was missing something.

When it comes to confession, perhaps you feel that you're missing something too.

So far we've seen that the secret to growing the authentic relationships we crave is repenting of our sin before God and experiencing his forgiveness—freeing us to be honest about our struggles with others. But how do we actually go about the *practice* of repentance?

Most of us struggle in this area. You might be like young Catherine, going through the motions of a routine without feeling the weight of sin. Maybe you're trying to drum up some sense of sorrow that isn't there. You know Christians are meant to feel sorry, but if you're honest you don't, really—at least not very often. How are you meant to repent when you don't feel repentant?

Or maybe you do feel sorrow and guilt over your sin. So you confess it to God, and then confess it again, and again—but you're not sure you're saying or doing the right things, because the guilt never seems to go away. Or you keep sinning in the same way, and you wonder whether God is losing patience with you.

Or maybe you're miserable under the weight of sin you haven't confessed, but you don't know where to start. How can you possibly come before God with this?

Or maybe you've just never given a lot of thought to confessing your sins, and this is all sounding pretty new.

Often we look at repentance as a statement—an "I'm sorry, please forgive me" that checks a box and (hopefully) alleviates our guilt. But in this chapter we'll look at Psalm 51 and see that repentance is a turning away from sin and a turning toward God—a process that doesn't merely alleviate guilt but cultivates deep joy. And that's not the only pay-off. Remember, repenting and receiving forgiveness from God leads to real relationships with others, because it reminds us that we've got nothing left to hide.

The compiler of the Psalms tells us that David wrote this prayer after his sin with Bathsheba. When I read his words, I realize how lacking my childhood confessions were. Actually, even many of my confessions in adulthood leave much to be desired. But by approaching God as David does, we can grow a habit of healthy confession that draws us from sorrow to joy—wherever we're coming from and however we've sinned. Here's how:

## 1. DEFINE SIN

*Have mercy on me, O God,*
*    according to your unfailing love;*
*according to your great compassion*
*    blot out my transgressions.*
*Wash away all my iniquity*
*    and cleanse me from my sin.*
*For I know my transgressions,*
*    and my sin is always before me.*          *(v 1-3)*

The first step to meaningful confession is understanding what sin is. David uses three different words for it here: "Iniquity," "sin," and "transgressions." We might assume that David has simply improved his poetry by using a thesaurus. But each term has been deliberately chosen for its unique meaning in Hebrew.

"Transgressions" implies a rebellion against God's authority and law—as the loving Creator, God has the right to set the rules for life in his world. But in sleeping with Bathsheba, David cast those rules aside.

"Iniquity" means a distortion of what should be. We were created to live in a way that brings glory to God—revealing something of his greatness by reflecting his good character to the world around us. But in iniquity we put ourselves at the center of our universe, using people and things to make ourselves look great instead.

"Sin" is a missing of the mark. God is wholly and totally perfect; we fall woefully short.

In this prayer, David is making it clear that his sin is deep—there is no minimizing or excusing it. And we need to admit the same thing. As you pray in repentance, thinking of a particular sin, admit to God...

- the way in which this was a rebellion against God's rule.
- the way in which this put you in the center of the universe, in place of God.
- the way in which you've fallen short of his holy standards.

You might find this quite hard. Perhaps you don't share David's overwhelming sense of guilt when he says, "My sin is always before me" (v 3). If that's the case, you need to ask the Holy Spirit to reveal the true weight of your sin to you. You could pray these words from David's prayer in Psalm 139:

*Search me, God, and know my heart;*
*    test me and know my anxious thoughts.*
*See if there is any offensive way in me,*
*    and lead me in the way everlasting.*      *(v 23-24)*

## 2. APPEAL TO GOD'S MERCY

Next, David appeals for forgiveness based on what he knows about God's character: that God is merciful. David knows that God is committed to him in a relationship (or covenant) of "unfailing love" (Psalm 51 v 1).

So David prays, "Blot out my transgressions" (v 1). I have off-white carpet in my dining area, and I am very clumsy... You can imagine how that works out. When there's a spill, my first step to cleaning it up is to grab a rag and to push it down on the spot to blot it out. Of course, what happens then is that the stain is transferred to and absorbed by the rag. "Blotting" carries with it this image—the transfer of a stain. In this prayer, David gives a Spirit-inspired image of what Christ would do in taking upon himself the stain of our rebellion: although we are guilty, Jesus' death on the cross absorbed the anger that we are due.

Next he asks, "Wash away all my iniquity and cleanse me from my sin" (v 2). One day when my kids were younger, my daughter thought it would be funny to make her little brother look like Sully, the big, hairy blue and purple monster from the Pixar film *Monsters Inc.* Her method included a lot of Crayola marker on his face. Unfortunately, it was not one of those "magic" washable markers. So I spent my afternoon scrubbing my son's face to get it to return to its natural hue. This is a bit of the image I get from this verse. If iniquity is a distortion of the way we were meant to reflect God's glory, then this is a request for God to change us deep down and make us new. God's image in us is marred and must be scrubbed clean.

- Ask God to have mercy on you; not because you deserve it, but because of his unfailing love for you.
- Acknowledge that God has transferred the stain of your guilt onto Christ.
- Ask God to cleanse your heart, scrubbing it clean so that you reflect his glory as you ought to.

## 3. AVOID DEFENSIVENESS AND SEE GOD RIGHTLY

*Against you, you only, have I sinned*
*    and done what is evil in your sight;*
*so you are right in your verdict*
*    and justified when you judge.*          (v 4)

David's sin hurt multiple people. He committed adultery, orchestrated a murder, and tried to cover it all up. And yet he says his sin is only against God. How can that be?

Well, if we think of sin as failing to hit the mark, then we have to ask, "Whose mark are we missing?" The answer, of course, is that it's God's mark. So although our sin does hurt others, and repenting to those people is important, sin is ultimately against God, since it's *his* ways that we have failed to live up to, and *his* image-bearers whom we hurt.

And since it's his law, he is justified in judging us and finding us guilty. The pastor of American poet Emily

Dickinson once told her, "You want to come to Christ as a lawyer, but you must come to him as a sinner—get down on your knees" (John Cody, *After Great Pain*, p 66). This is my tendency, too. I want to give my best defense. But presented with the reality of an all-powerful, holy God, there's no defense I can give for myself. I've done many things that are evil in his sight, and he is justified and blameless in his dealings with me.

- Admit that your sin is against God, and that he is right to be angry.

## 4. ACKNOWLEDGE THE DEPTH OF THE PROBLEM

*Surely I was sinful at birth,*
*   sinful from the time my mother conceived me. (v 5)*

Writers write, bakers bake, players play, and sinners sin. It's what we do. Sinclair Ferguson writes, "Evil deeds are the fruit of an evil heart. They are not an aberration from our true self but a revelation of it" (*The Grace of Repentance*, p 30).

David is not saying his conception was sinful, or that it's his mother's fault that he's a sinner. He's saying what's true of all of us: our sinful nature was present from the womb—we were born sinners.

So our sin is not just a "mistake" or a "slip-up." It's deep inside us.

Contrast that with the next verse:

*Behold, you delight in truth in the inward being,*
*and you teach me wisdom in the secret heart.*

*(v 6, ESV)*

David is sinful deep down, but God delights in truth deep down. And actually, this is what will combat sin. We need God's truth to work its way down into us, all the way into our "inward being." As Nancy Guthrie writes, "Sin flourishes when lies [about God] are cherished in the inward being" (*The Wisdom of God*, p 149). In the next few chapters, we will look at some of these lies and how to dismantle them. But for now, talk to God and…

- admit that this sin is a symptom of a deep problem with your heart.
- ask God to plant his truth in your heart and root out the lies.

## 5. LOOK TO JESUS

*Cleanse me with hyssop, and I will be clean;*
*wash me, and I will be whiter than snow.*     *(v 7)*

Hyssop was a plant with symbolic significance in the Old Testament. In Exodus 24 Moses used it to sprinkle blood from an animal sacrifice on the book of the law, the people, the tabernacle and all the vessels used for worship. In this way they were "cleansed" and made pure for God's service (even though they were covered with blood!) (Hebrews 9 v 18-21). The point was this: for forgiveness to happen, something or someone has to die.

So clearly, David's reference to hyssop here is not accidental. He knows hyssop signifies purification with blood, and he knows that blood alone can make him whiter than snow. What he doesn't know is *how* this will be done fully.

But we do. Instead of relying on an animal sacrifice, we look to Jesus, who "has appeared once for all at the culmination of the ages to do away with sin by the sacrifice of himself" (Hebrews 9 v 26). His blood is enough to make us "whiter than snow" (Psalm 51 v 7).

• Give thanks that Christ makes you pure by his sacrifice.

## 6. ASK GOD TO BREAK YOU AND HEAL YOU

*Let me hear joy and gladness;*
*let the bones you have crushed rejoice.*     *(v 8)*

The day before my seventh birthday, I was at gymnastics practice doing a routine back-walkover when something went wrong. Somehow, I had twisted my hand before putting my weight on it, and when I ended the trick, I looked down to see my right hand hanging down at an odd angle. Turns out I had what is called a "greenstick fracture." After x-rays at the hospital, the doctor explained that a fracture like this won't heal correctly unless the bone is broken all the way and then set. After two ineffective attempts to sedate me, the doctor asked my parents to leave the room and had me hold a nurse's hand with my good hand while he finished breaking my wrist. My path to healing had to come through more pain.

When God reveals our sin to us, it's similarly painful. David was already a sin-broken man; he just didn't fully realize it until God broke him all the way. It is God who breaks, God who sets, and God who heals.

And this is all mercy: 19th-century British pastor Charles Spurgeon wrote that seeing our weakness, and experiencing God's power to save, teaches us "a heart-music which only broken bones [can] learn ... [David] had been a mass of misery—mercy shall make him a mass of music!" (*Devotional Classics of C. H. Spurgeon*, p 290).

- Ask God to break your heart with the reality of your sin, so that you can rejoice fully at the healing he brings.

## 7. ASK FOR A RADICAL SOLUTION

*Hide your face from my sins,*
*and blot out all my iniquity.*
*Create in me a pure heart, O God,*
*and renew a steadfast spirit within me.*    *(v 9-10)*

It's not just my dining room carpet that gets dirty (see point 2). I don't think there's a room in our home in which I have not spilled coffee on the carpet. So, much to my non-caffeine-dependent husband's amusement, I have tried to strategically move furniture around to cover the various brown spots throughout our home. But my attempts to manage the stains can only go so far. Eventually, the carpet will need to be ripped up and replaced.

Perhaps this "move the furniture" plan is often the way you approach repentance. Many times, we're looking for a quick fix, as if it's just this one action that is our problem and we need a quick dose of forgiveness to relieve our guilt.

David has stopped with the furniture moving. He recognizes the scale of his problem. A holy God cannot look upon his sin. A quick fix will never take care of this. His heart is so wicked that he asks God to create in him a clean heart and a right spirit. What David needs—and what we need—is a miraculous act of renewal.

- Thank God that he has provided the deep solution your deep sin needs. Ask him to renew your spirit so that your heart's desire is to honor him.


## 8. BE COMFORTED BY THE SPIRIT

*Do not cast me from your presence*
*  or take your Holy Spirit from me.*  *(v 11)*

In the Old Testament, the Spirit equipped people who were anointed for a specific task (in David's case, ruling as king) and brought God's presence to them. But the previous king, Saul, had the Spirit "depart" from him because of his sin (1 Samuel 16 v 14). David does not want that to happen to him.

Yet the very fact that David is grieved over his sin is a sign that God's Spirit is at work in him. This is true for you as well. Have you ever been so discouraged by your sin that you've wondered, "How can God love me? Surely I'm not really a Christian." Take comfort in knowing that the very grief you're experiencing is a sign that you have the Spirit of God working in you, causing you to hate what God hates.

- Rejoice that despite your sin, the Spirit dwells in you, and will never be taken away.

## 9. REJOICE AND PROCLAIM TRUTH

*Restore to me the joy of your salvation*
  *and grant me a willing spirit, to sustain me.*
*Then I will teach transgressors your ways,*
  *so that sinners will turn back to you.*
*Deliver me from the guilt of bloodshed, O God,*
  *you who are God my Savior,*
  *and my tongue will sing of your righteousness.*
*Open my lips, Lord,*
  *and my mouth will declare your praise.   (v 12-15)*

David is like a bottle of soda that has been shaken—he needs only to be opened to burst forth and overflow with praise.

David is asking God to make him so joyful about his salvation that he can't help but teach other sinners the forgiving ways of God. This is important, because so often we do the opposite—we're inclined to wallow in our sin and draw back from serving others, whether in church or in our communities, because we think we're unworthy. But here David says the joy of forgiveness for sin should compel us to speak of that good news with friends, family, co-workers, and neighbors. Having experienced God's grace, we will want others to experience and rejoice in it too!

- Ask God to make you joyful over his forgiveness, and to use you to share that joy with others.

## 10. RESOLVE TO OBEY

*You do not delight in sacrifice, or I would bring it;*
*    you do not take pleasure in burnt offerings.*
*My sacrifice, O God, is a broken spirit;*
*    a broken and contrite heart*
*    you, God, will not despise.*
*May it please you to prosper Zion,*
*    to build up the walls of Jerusalem.*
*Then you will delight in the sacrifices of the righteous,*
*    in burnt offerings offered whole;*
*    then bulls will be offered on your altar.    (v 16-19)*

David can't make up for his sin with an animal sacrifice. While the sacrificial system was set up by God, it had its limits. It was a symbol that pointed to God's provision of the ultimate sacrifice: his Son. But even for Old Testament believers, going through the motions alone was not what counted; it was the heart with which they were done that mattered.

Sometimes we just "go through the motions" too—like the nighttime confessions I spoke across the hall to my brother. We can check all the boxes, do all the steps above, and say all the right words, but if in the back of our minds we're planning to sin in the same way again, then grace isn't truly taking root. What God desires is the mark of true repentance—a heart that is broken by sin.

As Puritan pastor and writer Thomas Watson wrote, "Till sin be bitter, Christ will not be sweet" (*The Doctrine of Repentance*, p 63). If we come to God with a heart like that, he "will not despise" it; he will accept it, and accept us, because of Christ's sacrifice on our behalf (v 17). Then we can get on with obeying God—together, as his people—in a way and with an attitude that delights him (v 19).

- Rejoice that God does not "despise" your broken heart. Thank him that you can delight him with your obedience.
- Ask him to "build up" you and your whole church family, so that you all live in a way that honors him.

## JOURNEY INTO JOY

True repentance is not a joyless, wallowing-in-sorrow repentance. It's a process that starts with grief and guilt, and ends with forgiveness and deep joy.

I learned that for myself one Wednesday morning in the auditorium of my small Christian college. I was standing in the back row during our mandatory chapel service. On the days when I managed to wake up and make it to our ten o'clock service, I generally enjoyed participating in the song worship. But on this day, I struggled even to stand with my friends and wait for the music to end.

My sin was before me, and this time rather than fearing disappointing people, I knew I could not stand in worship of a holy, gracious, loving God with unconfessed sin in my heart. I had been dishonest with someone, months prior to this particular Wednesday, and for some reason the Holy Spirit's conviction was heavy to the point that I knew I had no other choice than to repent before the Lord and then go immediately to the person to whom I had lied to confess and ask his forgiveness.

I still remember the freedom of walking away from that meeting with my burden lifted, able once again to sing and worship. For months, I had made excuses about this situation, but on this day the Lord's hand graciously pressed me to the point of calling my sin what it was and taking it to the cross, where it rolled off my back and onto Christ. My repentance before God led to a repaired relationship with another. And oh, the sweetest worship came as a result.

So what sins are weighing on your heart? What guilt have you been trying to cover with distraction? Or are you submerging yourself under the weight of it as a form of penance, rather than taking your sin to the cross, where it's already been paid for?

Take some time now to work through the steps above, and rejoice in the incomparable grace offered to you in Christ!

## REFLECT

- Can you think of a "watershed confession moment" from your life? Why is confessing sin to others so terrifying?
- How does understanding the terms "transgressions," "iniquity," and "sin" change the way you think of your failure to obey God?
- What word picture or analogy ("blot out," "wash away," "hyssop," "broken bones," etc) stands out to you from this chapter? Why?
- For some people, sorrow over sin comes easily, but it's harder for them to believe they're truly forgiven. Others find it easy to believe in forgiveness, but harder to understand the full weight of God's love because they aren't sorrowful over their sin. Which is your tendency? How does this chapter encourage you?

# 5. YOUR ROOTS ARE SHOWING

We bought our first home eight years ago. It's a sweet little place on a cul-de-sac filled with neighbors from other countries, and we love it. But when we moved in, there was zero landscaping: no plants, shrubs, or flowers. My grandmother and her best friend, a master gardener, came to the rescue and planted beautiful plants, shrubs, and flowers throughout the yard. Our bare patch of grass was transformed into an oasis.

A few months later, we were in the middle of one of the hottest summers on record in Nashville, Tennessee, and I was due to have a baby in August. I spent many summer days sitting in a tiny child's swimming pool in the backyard while my young daughter dumped buckets of water on me. Needless to say, pulling weeds just didn't happen, nor did watering the newly planted shrubs and flowers.

Unsurprisingly, some of them didn't make it through the summer.

From that moment on I determined to take good care of the remaining plants. Which I have, mostly... until last year. Life was busy, and I never got around to laying mulch. I pulled some weeds, but mostly cut them off at ground level, rather than worrying about the roots. Still, things looked decent from the outside.

But underground things were different. This year, my dad came to help me with the weeds and mulching, and what we found was shocking: an immense weed root system ran throughout whole flower beds. I would start pulling in one area, and soon I was holding five feet (1.5 meters) of a root system I couldn't find the end of. It's possible these roots had taken hold years ago, and my neglect had allowed them to take over completely. The visible weeds were growing all over the place because the roots had been spreading for years.

Sin is like those weeds. Sometimes our sin is so obvious we can't miss it, but more often we have hidden sin that even *we* don't realize is there. And the sin we *do* see—the more obvious expressions of laziness, anger, boasting, envy, judgmentalism, etc—are often indications that more is going on under the surface in our hearts. As in my garden, it's futile to try to deal with weeds without digging up the root.

In his book *Repentance: A Daring Call to Real Surrender*, the late pastor Jack Miller differentiates between "branch sins" and "root sins" (p 33). The insight is that branch sins are those deeds we commit that affect our relationships—the ones others see in us most readily. But root sins are the real issue. The root bears itself out in the branches. So if you want to repent of your sin in a way that leads to lasting change in your relationships, you need to dig deeper.

In Psalm 51, we saw David talk not about the sexual sin and murder, but about the bigger picture of sin before God. He knew his actions were only symptoms of a deeper issue. So, when he came before God, he dealt with the root. And as we look again at his example, we'll be helped to root out our sin and get real with others.

## THE ROOT OF DAVID'S SIN

To understand the root of David's sin, we need to step back and take in the bigger picture of his relationship with the Lord. In the book of Psalms we can find song after song written by David that praises and thanks God for his blessings. Take, for example, Psalm 16:

*Keep me safe, my God,*
  *for in you I take refuge.*
*I say to the LORD, "You are my Lord;*
  *apart from you I have no good thing."*
*I say of the holy people who are in the land,*
  *"They are the noble ones in whom is all my delight."*
*Those who run after other gods will*
  *suffer more and more.*

*I will not pour out libations of blood to such gods*
   *or take up their names on my lips.*
*LORD, you alone are my portion and my cup;*
   *you make my lot secure.*
*The boundary lines have fallen for me in*
   *pleasant places;*
   *surely I have a delightful inheritance.*
*I will praise the LORD, who counsels me;*
   *even at night my heart instructs me.*
*I keep my eyes always on the LORD.*
   *With him at my right hand, I will not be shaken.*
*Therefore my heart is glad and my tongue rejoices;*
   *my body also will rest secure,*
*because you will not abandon me to the realm*
   *of the dead,*
   *nor will you let your faithful one see decay.*
*You make known to me the path of life;*
   *you will fill me with joy in your presence,*
   *with eternal pleasures at your right hand.*

In this psalm, David gives us a picture of what it looks like to enjoy being one of God's people: he has a glad heart, a sense of security, fullness of joy, the promise of pleasures forevermore, the path of eternal life, God's personal counsel and instruction, a refuge in times of trouble. No wonder David says, "My whole being rejoices" (v 9, ESV). David's life was a joyful one, even in the trials and attacks he faced, because his joy was in experiencing God's faithful love.

But Psalm 51 v 12 is a stark contrast to these words—and it might just reveal the root of David's sin:

*Restore to me the joy of your salvation.*

David says he has lost the joy of God's "salvation"—the great pleasure of being chosen as one of God's people, enjoying the benefits of his love and special protection. This does not mean he has lost his salvation. Nathan assures David that the Lord is still committed to him as his chosen king of his chosen people, the Israelites (2 Samuel 12 v 13). God is faithful to his covenant promises. Yet David's joy in that relationship is gone.

I have always assumed David lost this joy as a result of his adultery. He felt far from God because of his sin and wanted to have the sin dealt with so he could have joy again. And no doubt this is true. But it seems there is more to it. Perhaps he lost his joy before this chain of events ever started. When God spoke to David through the prophet Nathan in 2 Samuel 12, he recounted all the things he had done for David and all he had given him, and said, "If all this had been too little, I would have given you even more. Why did you despise the word of the LORD by doing what is evil in his eyes?" (v 8-9)

It seems that David was looking elsewhere for joy, rather than in God and in his relationship with him—in a word, in salvation. The Hebrew word for salvation in Psalm 51 v 12 is *yesha*, which means "liberty, deliverance, prosperity." It comes from a word that means "to be open, wide, or free." This is the David we see in Psalm 16, but not in Psalm 51. The David of Psalm 51 has been enslaved to his desires and passions, rather than rejoicing in the freedom of God's salvation.

In *The Problem of Pain*, C.S. Lewis wrote, "I think we all sin by needlessly disobeying the apostolic injunction to 'rejoice' as much as by anything else" (p 61). In other words, we sin because we do not rejoice. I think this is why David prays, "Restore to me the joy of your salvation." When our deepest joy and happiness is found in relationship with God, all other passions and desires pale in comparison. But when we stop rejoicing in him, we start rejoicing in other things.

We see this in the New Testament in 2 Peter 1. Peter lists some of the good qualities that belong to those who are called by Christ—virtue, knowledge, self-control, steadfastness, godliness, brotherly affection, and love. Then he says, "For if you possess these qualities in increasing measure, they will keep you from being ineffective and unproductive in your knowledge of our Lord Jesus Christ. But *whoever does not have them is nearsighted and blind, forgetting that they have been cleansed from their past sins*" (v 8-9). So, if we lack these godly qualities, the problem is a form of spiritual amnesia—we've forgotten the gospel of grace, by which we are "cleansed." Forgetting what Christ has done for us leads to ineffectiveness; losing the great joy of our salvation leads us to sin.

The problem is we forget who God is—loving, faithful, good, and in sovereign control over all our circumstances.

We forget we are loved. We forget the lengths to which God went to redeem us and adopt us as his children.

In his actions with Bathsheba, David goes after something God has not given him. And why would he do that if he believed God truly loved him enough to give him every good thing?

The same is true with us. We either taste and see that the Lord is good (Psalm 34 v 8), or we go after other tastes and sights we think will satisfy. We either trust that our Father is truly loving, good, and sovereign, or we doubt that and attempt to get what we think we need on our own. We are like David or the wolf from the children's book *My Lucky Day*—so distracted by our appetite for other things that we overlook the far greater joy we already possess.

### HOW TO GET ROOTED

So what do we do about this? Paul shared some words with the church at Colossae that are helpful for us here. In this letter, Paul writes to the Colossians to encourage them in their faith and to deal with false teaching that has infiltrated the church. These verses sum up the heart of the book:

*So then, just as you received Christ Jesus as Lord, continue to live your lives in him, rooted and built up in him, strengthened in the faith as you were taught, and overflowing with thankfulness.*

*(Colossians 2 v 6-7)*

There's that word again: "root." This is a description of flourishing—rooted, built up, established, abounding. You might use those words to describe a healthy, fruitful plant. And look at what Paul tells the Colossians they will abound in as they walk in Christ: thanksgiving.

Paul talks more about this idea in Colossians 3. He starts by telling the Colossians…

> *Since, then, you have been raised with Christ, set your hearts on things above, where Christ is, seated at the right hand of God. Set your minds on things above, not on earthly things. For you died, and your life is now hidden with Christ in God.*
>
> *(Colossians 3 v 1-3)*

Then he goes on to tell the believers to "put to death … whatever belongs to your earthly nature": a list that includes immorality, evil desire, idolatry, anger, slander, and filthy language, among other things (Colossians 3 v 5-8). This is radical talk. Because these Christians "died" in Christ when Christ died on their behalf, they must put to death the old way of living. Their identities have been completely changed. Imagine a foreign spy who must take on a completely new identity, putting aside everything that was once part of his life, and embracing instead the traits of the person he has now become. Only what is required here by "putting to death" the old way is not just pretending to be a different person. It's an actual identity change, from the inside out.

So, like the Colossians, we must "put off" what belongs to our old identity, and instead put on the characteristics Paul lists later in this chapter:

> *Therefore, as God's chosen people, holy and dearly loved, clothe yourselves with compassion, kindness, humility, gentleness and patience. Bear with each other and forgive one another if any of you has a grievance against someone. Forgive as the Lord forgave you. And over all these virtues put on love, which binds them all together in perfect unity. Let the peace of Christ rule in your hearts, since as members of one body you were called to peace. (Colossians 3 v 12-15)*

These are instructions to the Colossian believers for living together as a "body"—a church family. New identities don't just affect the way we relate to God, but also to one another. Paul calls these Christians to put off their self-absorbed earthly ways, and instead to put on what will build up and serve others. And if you're anything like me, you look at that list and know that your heart doesn't match up.

Then notice the theme of the next verses:

> *And be thankful. Let the message of Christ dwell among you richly as you teach and admonish one another with all wisdom through psalms, hymns, and songs from the Spirit, singing to God with gratitude in your hearts. And whatever you do, whether in word or*

*deed, do it all in the name of the Lord Jesus, giving
thanks to God the Father through him.*

*(Colossians 3 v 15b-17)*

Three times Paul talks about being thankful. The Greek word here describing thankfulness is tied to the word for grace. This is a joyful gratitude for an undeserved gift.

This is a call to set our minds on God's ways, since this is what characterizes someone with a new identity in Christ. And this is possible because we're rooted in him. Just as a maple sapling, rooted in healthy soil, can only grow into a maple tree, a Christian rooted in Christ will grow up into the image of him. And such a Christian will be characterized by a life of thankfulness—even rejoicing—for the grace she has been shown; this is what will help us to clothe ourselves with kindness, compassion, humility, patience and love.

### SWEET, NOT SALAD

Somehow, though, when I read that I should seek the "things above" (Colossians 3 v 2), it sounds vague and, if I'm honest, unexciting. It's a bit like how nutritionists claim that eating sugar makes you crave more sugar, but once you stop eating it, eventually your body doesn't crave it anymore. Friends have told me this after they've done a detox, and I almost believe them—until I see their eyes staring longingly at a pastry or ice cream.

The problem is that if I think the world is sugar but the "things above" are something like salad, then I've already lost that battle. I'm only eating a salad because I know it's what's best for me and I'll feel guilty for eating sugar. But I'm not going to really delight in a salad.

But the "things above" are not salad. Psalm 34 v 8 says, "Taste and see that the LORD is good; blessed is the one who takes refuge in him." When I see the things of earth as more pleasing than Christ, it's probably because I'm not really tasting and seeing him. It's not about making something that doesn't taste good somehow less gross; it's about digging deep and maybe tasting truly for the first time. It's about returning again and again to the spring of living water—Jesus, revealed to us in the Bible and made dear to us by the Holy Spirit. When we truly taste and see that he is good, other things start to lose their appeal.

But the Holy Spirit is not a fairy godmother, appearing with a wand to instantly change our sinful desires into godly ones and then disappearing again. Rather, as we engage with Scripture and spend time with God in prayer, the Spirit transforms our desires and makes us more like Christ:

> *Now the Lord is the Spirit, and where the Spirit of the Lord is, there is freedom. And we all, who with unveiled faces contemplate the Lord's glory, are being transformed into his image with ever-increasing glory, which comes from the Lord, who is the Spirit.*
> *(2 Corinthians 3 v 17-18)*

As the Spirit shows us Christ, our hearts grow to love him more, and the taste of sin loses its appeal in light of a far greater joy. This means that the simple act of studying your Bible is an act of war against your sinful desires.

We have to remind ourselves to taste and see over and over again, because we're so quick to believe something else will satisfy. But we don't really have to convince ourselves that Christ is better. We just have to taste and see—and we'll find that he is.

## SIGHT OBSCURED

But here's the problem—often something gets in the way.

Several years ago, my husband and I went to London for a few days. There was a play I really wanted to see, but tickets were very hard to come by because Judi Dench was performing in it. So I kept checking the theatre websites, and there were a handful of seats available, but they were "obstructed view" seats. Basically, this means that you're sitting under the balcony, right behind a large pole. If we went to this show, we would spend the evening staring at a pole, rather than the play. There would be something amazing going on, but our sight would be obscured.

When our vision of Christ is obscured, it's usually because of things we have placed in the way.

Sometimes these obstructions are sinful things. The 18th-century English poet Alexander Pope wrote this about sin, or "vice", in *An Essay on Man*:

*Vice is a monster of so frightful mien,*
*As to be hated, needs but to be seen;*
*Yet seen too oft, familiar with her face,*
*We first endure, then pity, then embrace.*

This is talking about the normalization of sin. When we see it at first, we hate it. But the more we see it, the more we become accustomed to it, until eventually we embrace it. So rather than setting our minds on Christ, we divert the eyes of our heart to "earthly things." And over time, we like what we see.

Sometimes the things that obscure our sight of God are good things. But as the saying goes, "When a good thing becomes a God thing, that's a bad thing." We are so easily distracted. It's easy to lose the joy of God's salvation when our view of him is obstructed, regardless of the merit of what obstructs it.

So what is obscuring your sight of Christ at the moment?

In this season of life, for me it's been travel. I love to travel—to different countries, to the mountains, to the beach, to Disney World. You name it, I want to go. I visit travel-discount websites daily, check my credit card points to see where I can go, and mentally plan dream vacations. It brings me so much joy to share new experiences with my children, and to see their faces light up with the joy of a new taste or sight or sound.

But there's a darker side to all these travel dreams. I've struggled against envying friends who are traveling to places I'd love to go to. I've not been content with the circumstances in which God has placed me right now. I've resented people who earn more money than us and wondered why God won't give us more. And, unchecked, these symptoms spread and grow until I can't focus on anything else.

So what can I do? Well, I could get off Instagram so I don't have to see friends' travel pictures. And I could block travel sites from my phone and computer. I could implement a strict budget to save for a travel goal. These things might be wise. But ultimately these are all ways to treat the symptoms, or branch sins—they won't get to the root.

And what is the root? I've lost sight of Christ as the source of true joy. I start to think I need something else. I don't believe God is actually doing what is best for me.

Instead, right now I'm fighting a daily battle to focus on tasting and seeing the goodness of the Lord. I must remind myself of what is true—that God does not withhold *from* me anything that is good *for* me. That he is preparing for me something immeasurably more amazing than any vacation I can imagine—eternity with him. I have to practice gratitude for what he has given me and the ways in which he has proven his faithfulness over and over in my life. These are small, daily actions that gradually pull up the roots of these weeds that threaten to steal my joy.

Travel may not be the temptation for you. And truthfully, it's only one of many I struggle with.

A helpful question to ask yourself is to fill in this blank: *I'll be happy when...*

... I get a new job.

... I have a husband or child.

... my kids are more independent.

... I make better friends.

... my gifts are better used.

What would you put in the blank?

Again, none of these things are bad. In fact, these are good desires. But when we start to believe we will only be happy or have joy when those things happen, it's a sign that we're not seeing Christ as the source of joy. Instead, we're worshiping his gifts—idolizing things that can never satisfy us.

Or think of it this way: what truth about God do you struggle to believe? Is it hard to trust that he's good? Sovereign? Loving? Faithful? Forgiving? Do you rejoice in his salvation, or have you tucked that away, going back to living life as usual?

What is obscuring your sight of him? Will you ask him to show you?

Setting our minds on things above is an act of attentive gardening: putting sinful desires and actions to death before they can take root and spread. When I let the weeds go, assuming they're not that bad, it won't be long before I'm pulling up a complex and immense root system that has taken away my joy in Christ.

## FIND STRENGTH FOR THE STRUGGLE

In Chapter 7, we will talk more specifically about how we can fight our sin, knowing that so much of it stems from a failure to believe and rejoice in God's grace and love for us.

But the truth is, until we're with Christ in heaven, we will continue to struggle with sin. Jack Miller wrote, "What we must see is that God never promised to transform us into super-Christians who would never again sin and never again need to repent. He never promised anybody strength apart from continued dependence upon himself (Jeremiah 10 v 23; John 15 v 5)" (*Repentance*, p 43).

You will struggle, but Christ will be your strength. This is why repentance is a big deal—you need to repent daily because you will sin daily. But the same God who gave you faith to believe initially will continue to keep you and forgive you and strengthen you. The same God who mercifully forgave David is the God who forgives and loves you.

The weeding process can be long and humbling—but it's worth it. We're being transformed into a beautiful garden. And as that happens, our friendships grow and flourish too. As Christ roots out our fear, we open up more honestly; as he digs up our selfishness, we listen more carefully; as he tears out our pride, we speak more gently; as he unearths our envy, we love more sincerely.

When we pray for eyes to see the roots of unbelief in our hearts, he is faithful to show us, to forgive us, and to strengthen us by his Spirit. And that happens as he invites us to simply taste and see that he is good.

## REFLECT

- Do you daily rejoice in God's salvation? If not, what keeps you from doing that?
- What does it mean to "taste and see that the LORD is good"? How can we do this more?
- What obscures your sight of Christ? How did you fill in the blank: *I'll be happy when*…?
- Is there a Scripture verse or passage that stood out to you in this chapter? In what way?

# 6. TRUE AUTHENTICITY: STRUGGLING TOGETHER

*D*uring the opening credits of the 2002 movie *About A Boy*, the character played by Hugh Grant—Will—watches the gameshow *Who Wants to Be a Millionaire?* The question posed to the contestant is, "Who wrote the phrase, 'No man is an island'?" Will turns off the TV (while incorrectly guessing "Jon Bon Jovi" as the answer), and says he disagrees with the quote, because...

*All men are islands. And what's more, this is the time to be one. This is an island age. A hundred years ago, for example, you had to depend on other people. No one had TV or CDs or DVDs or home espresso-makers. As a matter of fact, they didn't have anything cool. Whereas now, you can make yourself a little island paradise.*

Will thought it was easy to be an island back in 2002. If only he could see us now! Now we have groceries delivered to our homes, a world of information and entertainment in our pockets, podcasts for sermons, and hundreds of online "friends" we never have to see.

My mom recently told me about a grocery store that would gather all my requested items for me and then bring them out to my car. My response? "But would I still have to talk to someone?" This "island paradise" idea is, I must admit, at times appealing to me.

It's never been easier to shut ourselves away, making "friends" online with people living hundreds of miles away, sharing the parts of our lives that feel safe and make us look good. But is this actually "paradise?"

## HIDE IT OR HATE IT

In the preceding chapters, we have talked a lot about repentance. We've looked at our desires and our distractions. We've looked at the ways we fail to rejoice in the Lord and how that leads to sin. And we've talked about confessing those things to God and repenting of them. But how do we put all those things together in a way that positively impacts our relationships?

Because, as the 17th-century poet John Donne (not Jon Bon Jovi) wrote, "No man [or woman] is an island" (*Devotions upon Emergent Occasions*, p 108-109). We weren't designed to go through life alone. The local church is God's gift to us—a diverse community for the building up of believers and the proclamation of the gospel to the ends of the earth. But sometimes we hide even from the people we see every week; we'd rather stay safe on our island than risk getting close to others.

This isn't what God wants for his church. As we saw in 1 John 1, God calls us to "walk in the light" together. James 5 v 16 says, "Confess your sins to each another and pray for each other." God calls us to be a community of honesty and grace. We know other people don't have the power to forgive our sins against God—that role is his alone. But what another believer can do is remind us of the forgiveness we receive in Christ. When we confess to another Christ-follower, and when that person prays for us, it's as if Christ is reaching through that person to extend fresh grace and mercy to us.

And confessing sin to one another helps us to change, too. In her book *Teach Us To Want*, Jen Pollock Michel writes, "The drive behind confession should not simply be the desire to admit my sin and relieve my conscience; the real motivation must be the will for holiness. Holiness can result from confession because speaking aloud our sin to another person is often the first step in beginning to hate it" (p 154).

So why don't we do this? Why do we instead spend our time together making small talk about our kids' schooling, or bemoaning our broken dishwasher, without ever speaking honestly about what's going on inside? Maybe you do. But for many, many years of my life, I didn't. Why not?

Sometimes we don't confess patterns of sin because we aren't ready to give them up. Augustine admitted praying as a young man, "Grant me chastity and continence. But not yet" (*Confessions*, p 145). In other words, he knew he eventually wanted to be rid of his sinful sexual desires—just not then! I know that if I give voice to a certain area I'm struggling with, I might be held accountable for it in some way; and sometimes I don't really want that.

For some of us, we are afraid. What will this person think of me if I tell her what's really going on in my heart? So we hold back, afraid to truly be vulnerable— trying to save face, or fearful of being rejected for not being quite enough. This plays into our pride. This is a big one for me. I want to look like I have it together, at least some of the time.

A few years ago, I watched the live action film *Cinderella* with my kids. There is a line at the end of the movie when the narrator says, "This is perhaps the greatest risk any of us will ever take—to be seen as we truly are." There is a good deal of truth in that. Of course, it's easy to take that risk when you're a good girl like Cinderella, whose only fault is that she's a simple (gorgeous) country pauper. It's a lot trickier when you're me: self-righteous, proud, judgmental, dishonest, impatient, discontent, greedy, lazy… and the list goes on.

I'm still very much a work in progress when it comes to vulnerability, swimming back and forth between the mainland and my island. But something changed for me a few years ago. So however you look on the inside, this kind of honesty is possible—and in this chapter, we'll see how.

## WHERE DO I START?

I am an introvert. I cannot handle lots of people for long periods of time. As I've mentioned, my idea of a dream vacation is myself, alone, in a hotel room. But thankfully, the Lord has given me two dear friends who pull me out of myself. One of these friends moved to my town a few years ago, and we immediately started spending regular time together. After the first few occasions, I noticed that whenever we met up she would ask, "How's your heart?"

The first couple of times I just said, "Oh, good, I think. Yeah. Nothing much going on." And then I turned it back on her and she told me some of the things she was struggling with. She eventually commented on how I was so laid back and must just not be dealing with much. She thought my marriage was perfect. She thought my kids must be angels.

Well, I didn't want to give her the wrong idea about things, so eventually I started preparing on my way to meet her, trying to figure out what I would say when she asked me. While my motivation was wrong, the effect was so good. I started actually examining my heart, praying for sin to be revealed, and then confessing it to another person. I had always analyzed everything around me, but tended to neglect my own heart.

The benefits of this friendship started to affect my other relationships. I was more open with my husband about my struggles because I was actually putting a name to them. I was quicker to admit failure and sin to other friends. And I was learning to hate those sins because I had spoken them aloud.

Vulnerability takes time and trust. I could trust my friend because I had spent time with her. I knew she cared about me. And I saw her own willingness to be vulnerable.

It takes time and trust—but it is worth it. Because ultimately, in relationship with other Spirit-filled, grace-loving believers, confession isn't about judgment and guilt; it's an opportunity to rejoice in the gospel.

Pastor Jack Miller writes of a Ugandan church that has "an unusual honesty in confessing their sins, and as a consequence the whole church has been filled with great joy. In practice this means that a grim-faced brother may be stopped on the street and asked by his fellow Christian, 'My brother, have you confessed your sins today? Have you seen the cross of Christ today?'" (*Repentance*, p 9-10).

Have *you* seen the cross of Christ today?

Because, as we saw in Chapter 5, the goal of repentance isn't just to identify sin. We must then take it to the cross and leave it there, rather than carrying it around with us.

If we're serious about doing repentance in community—about digging deep and supporting one another as we seek to walk in the light—we need to think about how best to go about it. Maybe as you're reading this, you're thinking of a friend or two whom you could ask to join you in this vulnerable endeavor. Who could you get into the habit of asking that question to: "How's your heart?"

But be warned: Satan doesn't want you to follow through. He would love for you to read this, think, "Oh, I should do that," and then either forget or downplay the need. Would you pray now that you would have the courage to seek out and build this kind of community? I promise you won't regret it.

## WHAT DO I SAY?

So what does it look like when we do start being honest with people—or when they start being honest with us? How is the rest of the conversation supposed to go?

We need to be careful to avoid two common, but unhelpful, responses.

The first is downplaying the sin. If you came to me and said, "Catherine, I yelled at my husband today," or, "Catherine, I'm really struggling with my attitude toward my boss," my instinct would be to say, "Oh, I'm right there with you. But give yourself grace—your husband isn't exactly perfect." Or, "Yeah, I get that. Your boss is the worst. At least you didn't actually say that to her."

Now the empathy is good. But ultimately, when I give those answers, I'm thinking about your opinion of me.

I don't want you to feel guilty, and I don't want you to think I'm being hard on you. I want you to like me and to think I'm a good friend.

The second unhelpful response is attempting to control the sin. Our instinct is to give advice: "Well, when I'm struggling with wanting to yell at my husband, I just count to five and think about my wedding vows." Or, "When my boss gets under my skin, I just try to think about something good about her. That really helps."

These are not necessarily bad ideas, but they don't get to the root of the problem. Instead, they make our problems with sin seem manageable: *If you just do this, you won't sin.* But as we've seen, the sin is not just the yelling or the bad attitude—it's the beliefs and desires taking root under the surface that are the real issue.

If we minimize sin or give each other "tips" to control it, we think we're giving each other grace, when in fact we're not. We're actually *denying* one another the grace we need by saying we don't need it. We should not deprive one another of sadness over our sin. When we deny the heavy reality of sin, and the "godly sorrow" that comes *before* repentance (2 Corinthians 7 v 10), we will also keep our friends from experiencing the joy that comes *after* repentance. The way we truly give grace to each other for our sin is by owning it, diagnosing it, and taking it to the cross. If there is true, overflowing joy to be found at the foot of the cross, then why would we stop our fellow believers on their way and tell them they don't need to go there after all?

So instead of minimizing sin or attempting to control it, we need to help each other get to the heart of where our desires are—where are we looking for joy? As we saw in Chapter 5, so much of our sin comes from believing that God isn't enough, and that what he gives us isn't enough. Instead of rejoicing in him, we rejoice in other gods. And when we chase after these idols, we break the other commands he has given.

We see this pattern in the shape of the Ten Commandments. When I worship the god of my own comfort and easy living, I will covet the people I see relaxing in their outdoor living rooms. When I worship the god of acclaim and reputation, I will lie when my reputation is threatened.

So don't make excuses, and don't give easy fixes. Instead, dig deeper together, because often we're blind to our desires. And sometimes we just need to process things out loud with others to help ourselves see what's really going on.

So if a friend says, "Catherine, I yelled at my husband today," my answer needs to point to truth and grace. I can say something like, "I know how that feels. The impulse to sinful anger is so strong, and I've done the same many times. But God is in the business of forgiveness and restoration. Have you repented to God and your husband? Remember, God's grace is sufficient. Can I pray with you for that relationship?"

Or if someone says, "Catherine, I'm really struggling with my attitude toward my boss," I need to not excuse it, but instead to say something like, "Some people are hard to respect and love. Why do you think that is? What is keeping you from loving your boss as yourself? If you're like me, you might be justifying your attitude because of your boss's behavior. Are there areas where you need to repent? How can I pray for you?"

It's worth saying that we also need to be prepared to have these kinds of honest (and sometimes awkward) conversations with the people we've hurt themselves. As we've looked at the story of David, we've seen the importance of confessing and repenting of our sin before God. But we also need to ask forgiveness from the people whom we've sinned against (Matthew 5 v 23-24).

I love the example of Zacchaeus, a hated tax collector who had charged people high tax rates so he could pocket the extra money. But when he meets Jesus, he is immediately changed. He responds to the love of Jesus by saying, "Look, Lord! Here and now I give half of my possessions to the poor, and if I have cheated anybody out of anything, I will pay back four times the amount" (Luke 19 v 8). The power of the gospel causes such a spirit of repentance in Zacchaeus that he doesn't just say, *I won't do this anymore.* Instead, he pursues justice and makes things right with those against whom he has sinned—not in order to somehow earn grace but because of the grace he's already been shown.

Sometimes we're tempted to just assume forgiveness from someone else, or to ask with no intention of seeking justice and healing. But the radical love of Jesus causes us to take our sin to the cross and then to pursue healing in our relationships with others, no matter what the cost to ourselves will be.

## WILL IT BE AWKWARD?

When my friend started asking me about my heart, it was awkward for me. I wasn't necessarily aware of a desire to hide anything—I just hadn't thought much about it. The thing about these kinds of friendships, though, is that the confession goes both ways. It's not like going through airport security, where the security agents can examine you and your baggage, whereas they get a free pass. That feels uncomfortable in a bad way. No, these friendships are meant to be two-way streets, where all parties willingly talk about their sin and then take one another's burdens to the Lord in prayer.

A few years ago, I started attending a women's Bible study where they did something they called "Walk in the Light." After their formal study time, the women divided into small groups and took turns asking and answering the question, "What in your life isn't working right now?" Basically, "In what areas are you struggling, or giving into sin?" Or, as my friend asked, "How's your heart?" Then one person would answer the question honestly, and when she was done, the other person would pray for her. No tips, no advice, no commentary—just prayer. Then they would swap roles.

When I first heard about this, I wanted to get up and leave before we even started (#introvertproblems). But

I figured that would be a little too obvious (#pride-problems). So, I stayed. And it was amazing. I had never met three of the five women in my group, but after 30 minutes of praying and sharing, we truly felt like sisters. And I knew more about them than I knew about many people with whom I'd been acquainted for years. I was confident that the information I shared would not leave that place, and I realized how desperate I was for my sisters to pray for me. The whole idea is straight out of 1 John 1, in which believers are urged to walk in the light and have fellowship.

So you may be thinking, "This sounds great, but how do I get this started? What if no one else does it? What if my friends think I'm weird?"

Of course, you can't force people to confess things against their will. But you can start by praying about being more open with those who love you. Creating these kinds of relationships often requires one person to step out and lead the way—and that person can be you. I never would have opened up in that setting, or with my friends, if someone else hadn't led the way. And yet, I realize now how much I would have missed without that act of loving service. By confessing their sin, others gave me the freedom to do the same, and I have experienced so much joy and healing because other people have prayed for me in my battle against specific sins.

And yes, it might be awkward at first. But it also might be one of the most loving things you can do for others, and for yourself. My friend Anna was the youngest member of our mixed-sex small group, unmarried in a group full of couples, and brand new to the group. Yet, at her first meeting she opened up not just about a difficult week or hard work situation but about discontentment. Her vulnerability gave me the nudge I needed to confess some things I had been struggling with, and even weeks later, that single act continues to encourage more honesty in our group.

I should say that in the desire and effort to create a space for vulnerability, we do need to guard against oversharing. Some people don't struggle with being vulnerable but instead with sharing too much. It can certainly be awkward, and even harmful, when someone opens up in ways that aren't appropriate for that setting. So how can we know if that's us? It probably comes down to our motives. Are we sharing in order to own up to our sin and move past it, or are we more concerned with what others think of us? Am I truly grieved over this sin, or do I enjoy the audience? Am I longing for others to speak of God's grace to me, or am I seeking their pity or their approval of my transparency? These are the kinds of questions that will help to guard us from sharing inappropriately.

## WHAT IF THEY'RE NOT SORRY?

Okay, so we might be okay with confessing our sin and asking others to pray for us, but what about when we see sin in someone else and they aren't repentant? Should we confront them? And how do we do it?

As with so many things in life, this is an area where the pendulum tends to swing to extremes. Pride either causes us to confront everyone in our paths, and not in a loving manner, or we overlook and ignore sin in others because we don't want to be seen as judgmental.

In Galatians 6 v 1-3, Paul writes about this topic, in a way which is as relevant now as it was then:

> *Brothers and sisters, if someone is caught in a sin, you who live by the Spirit should restore that person gently. But watch yourselves, or you also may be tempted. Carry each other's burdens, and in this way you will fulfill the law of Christ. If anyone thinks they are something when they are not, they deceive themselves.*

So, when we see a brother or sister caught in sin, we should restore him or her. How? "Gently." This verse comes on the heels of the passage describing the fruit of the Spirit, which includes gentleness. A Spirit-filled life will naturally lead to loving, hopeful, patient, and gentle confrontation of a fellow believer.

But note that Paul spends one sentence on the actual restoration, and then the next three sentences focused on the *person doing the restoration*. We're to watch ourselves, so that we don't, in our pride, also fall into that sin. We're to bear each other's burdens, rather than cast judgment. In other words, we don't look at someone else's sin as an opportunity to rejoice over our own holiness. When we truly appreciate Christ's work on our behalf, we know we have no room for pride—to feel otherwise is to deceive ourselves (v 3). And we don't just point out sin without doing something to help each other deal with it (v 2).

If, then, you see sin in a friend, the first thing you must do is pray—for the Spirit's leading, for conviction of wrong motivations in your desire to confront the other person, and for genuine love and concern for them. You need to first acknowledge your own blindness to sin. Then, you can go to that person and lovingly entreat them to repent and so experience the joy of forgiveness and restoration.

The role of being a "Nathan" in someone else's life is never one we should covet, and yet we all should want a Nathan to come to us when we're blind to our own sin. Of course, the best people to confront us are our closest friends. The confrontation of a stranger will rarely have the desired effect. Paul writes here to those in the local church, bound together by a common bond of love for Christ.

## BE A NATHAN, NOT A PRIEST

So we must avoid being judgmental—but there is also another danger to avoid here, and that's priesthood. That probably sounds weird, so let me explain.

In the Old Testament, the priest worked in the temple and acted as a go-between for the people and God. But for believers today, Jesus is our great High Priest, who provided access to the Father by his death on the cross.

This means that now, through Christ, all God's people are part of "a holy priesthood" with personal access to God (1 Peter 2 v 5). No one Christian has better or more intimate access than another—Christ is the only High Priest we need. That means it's dangerous to start depending on other go-betweens.

A few years ago, I started to spend time with another woman who had kids just a few years older than mine. We would have coffee, and she was a great listener and a wise person. She gave me great counsel, and I learned so much from her, including practical things like good books to read with my kids and how to cook extra crispy bacon.

But over time I started noticing something about myself. When I was talking to my kids, I started to think, "How would she say this?" Or when I snapped at my husband, I would think, "She would never do that." This friend was a godly woman—but I had made her into a kind of priest. I sought her wisdom and guidance, and thought of how she would do things. I would confess things I was struggling with, but I was trusting in her words and her opinion, rather than in Christ.

As we build a community of confession and repentance, we have to guard against setting up these "priestly" relationships. Jesus said, "Let anyone who is thirsty come to me and drink" (John 7 v 37). We don't need to go through a "priest"—we can go straight to Jesus. And we don't want people trusting in us when only Christ can satisfy their thirst. So it's wise to pray for protection against that, and to check our own hearts to see if we are either setting ourselves, or others, up as priests.

But we shouldn't let that keep us from seeking true fellowship with one another. Because God has brought us into his family, we have the joy of bearing one another's burdens—both the burdens of earthly sorrow and sickness and the burdens of sin. But the beauty of being a burden-bearer is that Jesus has already borne these things in himself:

> *Surely he took up our pain*
> *and bore our suffering,*
> *yet we considered him punished by God,*
> *stricken by him, and afflicted.*
> *But he was pierced for our transgressions,*
> *he was crushed for our iniquities;*
> *the punishment that brought us peace was on him,*
> *and by his wounds we are healed.*
>
> *(Isaiah 53 v 4-5)*

To bear another's burdens, all we have to do is go with him or her to the cross and lay those burdens down at the feet of the One who carried them for them. Confession and confrontation are, at heart, opportunities for freedom and joy. It's never too late to begin building the kind of friendships that will bring us back to the cross and help us to find our deepest joy in Christ.

## REFLECT

- The Ugandan believers ask each other, "Have you confessed your sins today? Have you seen the cross of Christ today?" What would be lost if they only asked the first question?

- How do we sometimes confuse making excuses for sin with "grace"? Is this a struggle for you? Why?

- Why is it such a temptation to look to other Christians as "priests"? Can you think of a time when you've done this, either with someone you know or with a figure on social media?

- What is one step you can take this week to pursue the kind of authentic relationships described in this chapter?

# 7. DEALING WITH SIRENS

*I*n summers during high school and college, I spent a good amount of time training for volleyball. A few friends and I would get together for workout sessions with a personal trainer several times a week.

It makes my muscles quiver just to think about it. It was not unusual for a trainee to run outside and vomit in the middle of a workout. Our trainer would blast '70s disco hits in a sweat-stench-filled basement, while we did rep after rep of leg presses, squats, and pullups. On my own, there's no way I would ever have willingly subjected myself to that torture. But when a friend called (or AOL Instant Messaged) to see if I wanted to go, I agreed, knowing we would be tortured together. In the middle of the workout, I would look over and see a teammate gritting through it, arms shaking, and it would spur me on. Pressing on together allowed me to accomplish things I never would have alone. The same is true in the Christian life.

So far we've thought about why we so often lack meaningful, honest relationships—because the shame of our sin makes us hide.

We've thought about how to deal with that sin—through a habit of regular repentance, not just for the "branch" sins but for the roots underneath.

We've thought about how confession looks in relationship—taking the lead in opening up to talk about sin—and the blessing of deeper relationships that come as a result.

But deeper relationships are not the end goal. Confession isn't a means to an end where the end is a warm fuzzy feeling because we've found the friends we've always wanted. Instead, deep Christian friendships are a gift from God to spur us on in following Jesus—to help us to keep turning from sin and toward Christ. When we confess our sin to others, we gain allies in the fight against that sin—because, much like my college volleyball workouts, we can fight sin better together than we can on our own. The whole thing works in a virtuous cycle:

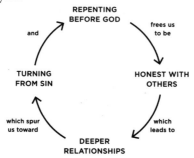

In this chapter, we'll look at two approaches to get serious in our struggle in community against sin. We'll call them the "Odysseus tactics" and the "Orpheus tactics," after two heroes from Greek mythology who both encountered Sirens. The Sirens were island-dwelling women whose enchanting voices lured sailors to their deaths. Once their melodies were heard, there was no resisting their charms, and many a crew met their demise as they were shipwrecked on the Sirens' island. But two crews managed to escape the danger of the Sirens through two different strategies. Let's consider them in turn.

## THE ODYSSEUS TACTICS

First up, Odysseus. When he was warned that he and his men would have to pass by the Sirens' island, he commanded the crew to put wax in their ears so they could not hear the song. But he wanted to hear it, so he had his men tie him with strong cords to the ship's mast. The words of the Sirens' song, promising knowledge and glory, were more tempting even than the music. But the ropes kept him safe from danger, the wax kept his crew on track, and the ship passed by unscathed.

Psalm 1 suggests we do something similar when it comes to the temptations of sin:

> *Blessed is the one*
> *who does not walk in step with the wicked*
> *or stand in the way that sinners take*
> *or sit in the company of mockers.   (Psalm 1 v 1)*

In contrast with the blessed person, the picture here is of someone who is gradually carried along by the tide of "sinners" who reject God—first walking alongside them on their way down the road; then stopping to chat for a while; then sitting down to enjoy their company. What we see is that our influences matter. Happiness and blessing come to the one who avoids a lifestyle that glorifies sin and wickedness, and who avoids the temptations that lead them in that direction.

This doesn't mean we should avoid any contact with people who aren't Christians—far from it. But it does mean that we need to take deliberate precautions to avoid being carried along by the tide of ungodly conversations or lifestyles. If we don't expect to stand out, we'll never stand firm. And while joining up with those who advise us to choose a wrong path or who mock God's ways will usually feel easier and even "freer", true happiness cannot be found there.

Like Odysseus' crew, we must be vigilant to avoid the Sirens' song of temptation—otherwise we will be carried away. As with those excruciating volleyball workouts, strength and health don't come from laziness, whether physical or spiritual. We have to identify the messages and temptations we face on a daily basis and take steps to avoid them.

There's wisdom in keeping ourselves from situations in which we know we'll be tempted. Why needlessly subject ourselves to things that are hard for us to resist? I don't go to the mall as much as I used to or watch home-improvement shows because I've realized I then start to look around at my closet or my home with dissatisfaction and covet what others have.

It's a sign of maturity when we begin recognizing what leads us to temptation, and take steps to avoid those things. This is something that we can do in community too. For instance, if you struggle with overdrinking or overspending, why not ask a Christian friend to come along with you to the party or on the shopping trip? Or if you know that your battle with lust is most intense at 9pm on a Friday night, why not ask someone to pray for you and text you at that time? Sometimes, like Odysseus, we need someone to tie us to the mast for our own protection.

And we need to be prepared to lovingly appeal to others when they're entranced by the Sirens' song. We need to be willing to graciously say things like, "I've noticed you seem to demean your [friend, spouse, child] when you're talking with other friends. Could it be that you're worried about what other people think and you're speaking out of insecurity?" Or, "I know lots of people watch that show you mentioned the other day. I've heard it's got lots of racy scenes in it. Sometimes those kinds of scenes can really affect me in ways I don't realize at first. Have you thought about why you're watching it and how it might affect you?"

But fighting sin in community won't always look like you expect. For example, when I was growing up, the idea of having an "accountability partner" was popular. This was someone you could meet with, and they would ask how you were doing in a certain area in which you were particularly tempted by sin. I think the idea of accountability, when done with love and humility, is a good one. But looking back, many times those relationships seemed more like either gossip sessions or self-help counseling.

True accountability involves a broken heart and a listening ear. In a grace-filled, hopeful accountability partnership, we will pray and fight together, knowing that repentance isn't a one-time deal and that some sins hang on tight. Sometimes we will struggle with a particular sin for ages—even for our whole lives. But love doesn't just leave me in my sin and excuse it. Love says, "I hate that there is still sin in the world, and I hate that it keeps ensnaring you. I am here to fight with you, to pray for you, and to encourage you in your fight."

This kind of accountability also encourages our hearts as we see prayers answered and battles won. We won't win every battle, but the Spirit does empower us to increasing obedience and fruitfulness.

For example, several years ago my husband confessed to me that he struggled with compassion for others, especially unbelievers. The Spirit had revealed this weakness to him. So together we repeatedly prayed for a change of heart.

And God has graciously answered that prayer. He is now one of the most compassionate, evangelistically-minded men I know, passionate about sharing the good news. My heart has been so encouraged by watching God answer that prayer, and I'm thankful Erik let me witness the transformation. Seeing God answer prayer in another person's life gives me hope in God's ability to change my own.

So what's it for you? My guess is that you too have areas of temptation you need to recognize and avoid. Is there a friend you can ask to help you? Because according to Psalm 1 v 1, avoiding these temptations leads to true happiness.

## THE ORPHEUS TACTIC

But Odysseus' method for dealing with the Sirens was not the only one, nor is it always the most effective. After all, any of the men could easily have removed the wax from their ears and steered the ship off course. We sometimes think we can control our hearts through behavior modification and rules, but that's just not the case. As we've seen, our best weapon against sin is rejoicing in something better than the siren song of the world around us.

This is what happened when the mythological musician Orpheus sailed with Jason and the Argonauts. They, too, had to pass by the Sirens' island. But Orpheus was so skilled on his lyre that his music roused the sailors when they were tired, comforted them when they were afraid, and drowned out the song of the Sirens. His music was so sweet that the Sirens' song lost its allure.

When we rightly view God as our loving Father and Creator, and when we meditate on his supreme worth, the joy we find in tasting and seeing his goodness will cause all earthly joys to fade. But it's not a one-time thing. This is a song we must repeat over and over again, to ourselves and to others, in order to drown out the allure of the world's song.

We see this in the next verse of Psalm 1:

> ... *but [blessed is the one] whose delight is in*
> *the law of the* LORD,
>   *and who meditates on his law day and night.*   *(v 2)*

The happy person does not delight in things that are opposed to God's word, but delights in meditating *on* God's word. The Hebrew word here for "meditate" is the same word used in Isaiah 31 v 4, which describes a lion growling over his prey (Eugene Peterson, *Answering God*, p 26). This is a different picture than one of just reading or thinking about Scripture. This is tasting, chewing, experiencing.

Delighting in the word of God is like soaking up the water of a stream and bearing fruit:

> *That person is like a tree planted by streams of water,*
>   *which yields its fruit in season*
> *and whose leaf does not wither—*
>   *whatever they do prospers.*                    *(v 3)*

This brings to mind another fruit-bearing plant—the vine in John 15. Jesus said:

*Remain in me, as I also remain in you. No branch
can bear fruit by itself; it must remain in the vine.
Neither can you bear fruit unless you remain in me.
I am the vine; you are the branches. If you remain in
me and I in you, you will bear much fruit; apart from
me you can do nothing.*       *(v 4-5)*

Much like the tree in Psalm 1, this is a picture of a plant receiving everything it needs and naturally bearing fruit due to its physical position in relation to nutrients. The streams of God's word in Psalm 1 are now the "Word made flesh" who speaks in John 15. And apart from him, we can do nothing.

But how do we abide or "remain" in Christ practically? This easily becomes a phrase that looks good on a coffee mug or as a print on our walls, but how do we actually do it? How do we tune in to sweeter music than the Sirens' song?

First, our ability to remain in Christ is due to God's grace and Jesus' work on the cross. This is Spirit-fueled fruit-bearing, due to his power and not our own.

But a key part of remaining is consuming what the Vine dispenses, like sap that runs from the trunk out through the branches. A little later Jesus says, "If you remain in me, and my words remain in you…" (v 7). The word of God is crucial to our remaining. We can't abide in someone we don't know, and we can't know him apart from the Bible. The nutrients of Scripture direct our choices and influence our affections. They cause us to see Christ as glorious and admirable above all other things.

In my life, things I've found helpful have included Scripture memory, placing verses about Christ's love on my walls, and listening to Scripture-filled music throughout my day. These are small things, but they're vital ways of fighting to remain in Christ, especially when the pull of the world's song is so strong.

So I know how this sounds—*Catherine, you're telling us to read our Bibles.* And yes, in fact, that's true. Nothing novel here. But in my life, God has used people delivering obvious messages to remind me of what I already know—that he has given me all I need for life and godliness (2 Peter 1 v 3). I just need to tap into it.

And that's our daily problem: we look to other things to satisfy us. We so easily forget that we have all we need in Christ. We distrust his goodness and seek the good we want on our own. Or we coast by, easily swayed by every message that sounds promising, rather than fighting to fill our hearts and minds with what is truly good. Instead, we must sing a better song in order to drown out the empty promises of the world.

And as with the sailors on Orpheus' ship, it usually helps when *someone else* sings it to us and with us.

That's the beauty of God's plan for his people. He is not making a bunch of individual Christians to go it alone—he is creating a *people*. When we join together on Sunday mornings to sing, take communion, and hear the word taught, we are recalibrating our hearts together.

One of my favorite books is *The Hiding Place*, the story of World War II prison-camp survivor Corrie ten Boom. Her father, Casper, was a watchmaker, and every week he would ride the train to Amsterdam to reset his watch by the official clock in that city. Then he would bring the time back home and set all his clocks and watches by it. A week later, he would go back again. This was just before the development of the technology that would allow clocks to keep accurate time without the need for constant resetting. So even in one week, the time would get off, and he would need to recalibrate the following week, and the next, and the next.

Our worship gatherings as a church are a chance for us to set our clocks by the true clock, as it were.

The book of Nehemiah tells of how the people of Israel returned to Jerusalem from exile and rebuilt the city walls. In chapters 8 and 9, the people gather to hear the reading of the Law of God—and then something strange happens. They are overwhelmed with grief over their sin. In response, their worship leaders lead them in praising God for his faithfulness and love, and in specific confession and repentance of their many sins. If you take a few minutes to read it, you'll see that the leaders don't shy away from detailing the ways in which they have, for generations, rebelled against God. And yet, in light of God's grace and faithfulness, they rejoice with a week-long celebratory feast.

The teaching of God's word has that effect on us. Encountering God shows us not only his holiness, but also our unworthiness. There have been many times when the Lord has used times of confession in weekly corporate worship to work on my heart. Your church may not have a structured time of confession, but even in the teaching of God's word, the Holy Spirit works to reveal sin to us—and ultimately, to remind us of the grace we have in Christ. We can use times of silence and reflection to confess sin and praise God for his grace. Together, we can sing and confess our sin through the words of our songs—admitting that we're "prone to wander" and in need of his "marvelous grace." And then we can rejoice together that...

> *My sin—oh the bliss of this glorious thought—*
> *My sin, not in part but the whole,*
> *Is nailed to his cross, and I bear it no more;*
> *Praise the Lord, praise the Lord, oh my soul!*
> *(Horatio G. Spafford, "It Is Well with My Soul")*

This is what it means to "let the message of Christ dwell among [us] richly as [we] teach and admonish one another with all wisdom through psalms, hymns, and songs from the Spirit, singing to God with gratitude in [our] hearts" (Colossians 3 v 16). So when we join together on Sunday mornings to sing, observe the Lord's Supper, and hear the word taught, we are being like Orpheus, singing a better song to one another than that of the Sirens. We are reminding one another of what is true, what is real, and what is of supreme worth. We are reminding one another that all those things we thought would satisfy us this past week truly won't. In this way we retune our hearts to the song of the gospel.

## WHEN SINGING THIS SONG IS HARD

So church is important—but it isn't always easy. I know that. A few years ago, I went through several months of off-and-on spiritual depression. I would sing in church and hear the gospel preached but had no joy. Some of this was because of conflict in relationships. I had been stripped of my faith in people, and I felt as if I wanted to walk away from the church as an institution. During this time I had a couple of breakdowns, suffered some depression, and wondered if any of what I believed was true at all. I didn't want God. I wanted to want him, but I didn't. And I felt that I couldn't.

Maybe you've been there, or you're there right now. Maybe you're reading this and doubting that you can really experience delight in God. Perhaps your circumstances feel too dark for joy. Perhaps God doesn't seem to delight in you, and when you read his word you don't taste and see his goodness—it just feels like work.

One of the things I learned during that time in my life was that I can't judge God's love for me based on my feelings and thoughts about him at any given moment. Praise Jesus, it doesn't work that way. He is faithful even when I'm struggling. His grace is sufficient even for that.

When I was going through those months of doubt and sorrow, I could do little more than read Psalm 42 over and over again.

Verses five and eleven both say,

> *Why, my soul, are you downcast?*
>   *Why so disturbed within me?*
> *Put your hope in God,*
>   *for I will yet praise him,*
>   *my Savior and my God.*

I held onto that: that one day I would again praise him—that I could hope in him.

And, by God's grace, it's true—that day has come.

## DEPENDENCE IS THE GOAL

As we do battle together—pressing on like Odysseus and Orpheus against the Sirens' song of temptation—we need to be careful that we're aiming at the right thing. Otherwise our relationships will descend into judgmentalism and pride, and we'll be right back where we started, trying to hide.

It's easy to think that sinlessness is our goal, and that it might be attainable on this side of eternity. But the picture we have in John 15—of the vine and the branches—is not one of perfection but dependence. God could easily have saved us and perfected us in the same moment, but instead we continue to be tempted and to fail.

The English slave-ship captain turned pastor John Newton wrote a good deal about our ongoing struggles with sin. He believed God purposefully uses our sin to remind us of our need for Christ, writing:

> *Experience is the Lord's school, and they who are taught by him usually learn that they have no wisdom by the mistakes they make, and that they have no strength by the slips and falls they meet with.*
> *(Advantages from Remaining Sin)*

In other words, we learn of our own wickedness and our need for God by experiencing our ongoing sin. Sometimes it's easy to think of ourselves as grade-A Christians, but God graciously teaches us of our need for dependence on him by allowing us to "slip" and "fall."

This attitude of dependence on Jesus strips us of competition and pride, which can so easily plague our relationships in the church. When we think it's up to us to be perfect, or at least closer to it than the next church member, we will refuse to open up about sin, and try to hide it instead. Or we'll give up on ourselves or others when not enough "progress" is being made. But when we recognize that we're utterly powerless without the Son of God dying on our behalf and the Spirit of God at work in our hearts, we will be honest with one another, choosing to help instead of hide, to confess rather than compete, and to persevere rather than quit.

## COMMUNITY IS COMING

The kind of community described here may seem impossible. You may be in a place where you can't imagine being accepted or feeling free to confess. Many churches and Christians have failed at this, myself included. In fact, you might be convicted now to confess your own judgmentalism and lack of compassion for fellow sinners. I have to confess that regularly.

If we're frustrated with our local church, our instinctive response is often to run away or build online communities where we share interests or backgrounds with one another. And there is joy in finding like-minded people around the world whom we can pray for and share our lives with.

But the local church is different. Our churches are not places where we hand-pick who can be in our community. We don't build a group based on interests. Our churches are a melting pot of believers from various backgrounds, with different tastes, desires, and gifts. We also have different sins that plague us. But we can all share in the joy of being sinners saved by a merciful God. When we start from this place, even those with no shared interests can develop deep, lasting community.

But the truth is that we can't sit back and wait for someone else to build this kind of community. Like my friends who persisted with me, we need to be the people who ask the awkward questions. Something as simple as "How's your heart?" or "What's threatening to steal your joy in Christ?" or "Would you pray for me about something and hold me accountable?" can begin to pave the way for truly being known and truly knowing. When we're willing to make these first moves, we will slowly start to see the Lord move and bring about repentance and joy in our churches and communities.

And as we do that, we will see the siren song of the world fade into the background as we embrace the far greater, sweeter song of our Savior.

How will you sing that song? How will you listen to it? And who will join you?

## REFLECT

- What are some "Odysseus tactics" you need to employ in your life?
- What are some "Orpheus tactics" you need to employ?
- What does it mean that "dependence is the goal?" Can you think of a time when you've seen your dependence on Christ?
- Spend some time praying about what you could do to help build a community that sings a more beautiful song together.

# EPILOGUE

*Then I saw "a new heaven and a new earth," for the
first heaven and the first earth had passed away, and
there was no longer any sea. I saw the Holy City,
the new Jerusalem, coming down out of heaven from
God, prepared as a bride beautifully dressed for her
husband. And I heard a loud voice from the throne
saying, "Look! God's dwelling place is now among
the people, and he will dwell with them. They will be
his people, and God himself will be with them and
be their God. 'He will wipe every tear from their eyes.
There will be no more death' or mourning or crying or
pain, for the old order of things has passed away."*

*He who was seated on the throne said, "I am making
everything new!"*       *(Revelation 21 v 1-5a)*

I remember a literature professor at my small Christian college discussing C.S. Lewis' book *The Great Divorce* with our class one day. He looked at me and said, "Catherine, in the new creation you will be your real, true self. Right now you're only a shadow of your true self. Then, you will be more real than you can imagine."

I was embarrassed at the tears that quickly filled my eyes. I thought I was already real—but in that moment, the longing I felt at this idea of being my real, true self showed that somehow I wasn't.

When we think about the eternity awaiting those who are "in Christ," we're usually drawn to the promises that there will be no more death, pain, or crying—no more suffering of any kind. We can scarcely imagine this kind of perfection. We have no real concept of a world without these things. Even as I write this, I'm burdened by the sudden death of a beloved former high school teacher and the news of a recent school shooting. This beautiful promise of no more death and pain and suffering gives me great hope.

But that's not the only thing we've got to look forward to. What will make us truly *real* in the new creation is that we'll be the people we were designed to be back in Genesis 1 – 2. Just imagine what that will be like:

- No hiding from others
- No covering up
- No faked smiles
- No frustrating shallowness when we're longing for depth

- No guilty feelings or sense of shame
- No fear that others will find us out

Why? Because there will be no sin. None. Ever.

Best of all, we will know Christ, face to face, and experience being fully known and loved by him as he wipes the tears from our eyes. And we'll have relationships with all God's people that are free of pretense and shame. Even the sweetest, most honest friendships we know now won't compare with the freedom and joy of relationships free of sin's effects.

In the daily struggle with sin, and in the daily challenge to be real about those struggles, nothing brings me joy like hope in God's enduring love and the promise that one day I will no longer have to strive against my sin. Right now, sin affects our lives every minute of the day. But we are not without hope. Even now, our Savior is making everything new. *Every* thing—including you.

So this is the reality in which we live now: looking to a future inexpressible joy, while spreading as much of that joy here as we can. This is our privilege—to be "joy-casters," sharing with our neighbors and friends what truly matters. As Paul writes in Colossians 3 v 2-4, "Set your minds on things above, not on earthly things. For you died, and your life is now hidden with Christ in God. When Christ, who is your life, appears, then you also will appear with him in glory."

I'm in a small group of women who gather on Saturday mornings to study Colossians together. One week, as we looked at this passage, a friend read from her New

Living Translation, which translates verse 3 as, "Your *real* life is hidden with Christ in God."

The sin that plagues you now is not your *real* life. Your real life is hidden and secure with Christ in God. If you've trusted in his perfect life, his sacrificial death, and his miraculous resurrection as the only way to be saved from the penalty for your sins, then you are *in* him. *He* is your life… your real life.

You are free to struggle against sin, and you're free to confess your sin to others because you have been forgiven. Nothing you do can change his love for you. So lay that burden of sin down, and then encourage others to do the same. Invite others to embrace their real lives.

And one day, you and I will experience true joy in the presence of our Father, unburdened by sin, surrounded by friends, and finally *real*.

> *He who testifies to these things says, "Yes, I am coming soon." Amen. Come, Lord Jesus.*
> *(Revelation 22 v 20)*

# FURTHER READING

Works referenced in each chapter are noted below.

## CHAPTER 1

- See Michael Reeves' excellent book *Delighting in the Trinity* (InterVarsity Press, 2012) for more on the idea of the fellowship of the Trinity.
- Brené Brown, *Daring Greatly: How the Courage to Be Vulnerable Transforms the Way We Live, Love, Parent, and Lead* (Gotham Books, 2012).
- The study by Brigham Young University can be found in Julianne Hold-Lunstad et al, "Loneliness and Social Isolation as Risk Factors for Mortality" in *Perspectives on Psychological Science*, Vol 10, Issue 2, 2015. See also https://news.byu.edu/news/prescription-living-longer-spend-less-time-alone (accessed April 18, 2018).

## CHAPTER 2
- Augustine, *Confessions. Translated by Henry Chadwick* (Oxford University Press, 2008).
- Timothy Keller, with Kathy Keller, *The Songs of Jesus: A Year of Daily Devotions in the Psalms* (Viking, 2016).

## CHAPTER 3
- https://tv.avclub.com/call-the-midwife-maybe-a-baby-1798174583 (accessed April 7, 2015).
- John Stott, *The Incomparable Christ* (InterVarsity Press, 2001).

## CHAPTER 4
- John Cody, *After Great Pain: The Inner Life of Emily Dickinson* (Belknap/Harvard, 1971).
- Sinclair Ferguson, *The Grace of Repentance* (Crossway, 2000).
- Nancy Guthrie, *The Wisdom of God: Seeing Jesus in the Psalms and Wisdom Books* (Crossway, 2012).
- Charles Spurgeon, *Devotional Classics of C. H. Spurgeon* (Sovereign Grace Publishers, 1990).
- Thomas Watson, *The Doctrine of Repentance* (Banner of Truth, 2012).

## CHAPTER 5
- C. John Miller, *Repentance: A Daring Call to Real Surrender* (CLC Publications, 2009).
- C.S. Lewis, *The Problem of Pain* (Harper Collins, 1996).

- Alexander Pope, *An Essay on Man* (Project Gutenberg), www.gutenberg.org/files/2428/2428-h/2428-h.htm (accessed March 25, 2018).

### CHAPTER 6

- John Donne, *Devotions upon Emergent Occasions* (University of Michigan Press, 1959), p 108-109. Originally published in 1624.
- Jen Pollock Michel, *Teach Us to Want* (InterVarsity Press, 2014).
- Augustine, *Confessions. Translated by Henry Chadwick* (Oxford University Press, 2008).
- C. John Miller, *Repentance: A Daring Call to Real Surrender* (CLC Publications, 2009).
- Eugene H. Peterson, *Answering God: The Psalms As Tools For Prayer* (HarperCollins, 1991).

### CHAPTER 7

- For more detail on the Greek mythology in this chapter, see Edith Hamilton, *Mythology: Timeless Tales of Gods and Heroes* (Penguin, 1969)
- The John Newton quote can be found online at www.gospelweb.net/JohnNewton/advantages-fromremainingsin_Prnt.htm (accessed December 3, 2017).

# ACKNOWLEDGMENTS

For someone who likes to believe she doesn't need help, writing a book is quite a humbling experience. It's no exaggeration to say that this book would not exist without many gifted people. And if it did exist, it would be a mess.

The team at The Good Book Company has been amazing. Thanks to Anne, Brad, Carl, Joe, Tim, and many others for your work to get the message of *Real* to the world. And I owe an enormous debt of gratitude to Rachel Jones. Your editorial vision and direction were such a comfort to me. Thanks for understanding the message and then greatly improving the delivery.

Thanks to Trillia Newbell for introducing me to TGBC and for your encouragement and real talk over the years.

Patti Hummel was one of the first to champion this message, and I'm thankful for the ways in which she helped me refine it.

Thanks to those who took the time to read the manuscript and give feedback: Jenny, Carol, Amber, Clair, Lisa, Mom, Dad, and Erik.

My Redemption City Church small group prayed me through the writing. I'm so grateful for the real community we've found with you all!

Saturday morning Bible study girls, you help me live out the words of this book. Thanks for being "real" with me and letting me be the same. Our time together has been a huge encouragement to me.

To Sophie and Micah, who receive the brunt of my sin and show immeasurable love and forgiveness daily, thank you. Your unconditional love is a constant example to me. You see the real me, and love me anyway. I love you both dearly.

Erik, thirteen years later, I'm still learning how to be real with you. But there's no one more gracious, patient, and gentle than you. Thanks for loving me deeply and sacrificially. I see Christ in you daily, and I love getting to grow in grace with you.

And without the grace of God displayed through the life, death, and resurrection of Jesus Christ, being real would be devoid of all hope. Praise God, we can love him because he first loved us, and we can experience the joy of true forgiveness.

# ENJOY GOD IN EVERY MOMENT OF EVERY DAY

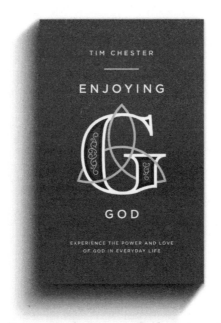

We believe in God, we serve God, we trust God, but would we say that we experience God on a day-to-day basis? Tim Chester explores what a relationship with God really looks like. As we see how the three Persons of the Trinity relate to us and how to respond, we will discover the key to enjoying God every day.

# RECOVER THE LOST ART OF GRATITUDE

Mary K. Mohler helps women discover the joy of a thankful heart as she unpacks Scripture to help us thank God for who he is as well as for his blessings, while overcoming obstacles along the way.

THEGOODBOOK.COM/GROWING-IN-GRATITUDE
THEGOODBOOK.CO.UK/GROWING-IN-GRATITUDE

# HURT IS REAL.
# BUT SO IS HOPE.

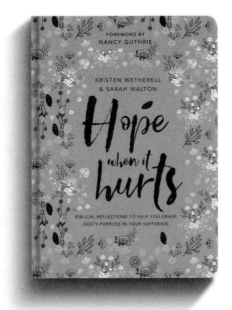

Kristen and Sarah have walked through, and are walking in, difficult times. So these thirty biblical reflections are full of realism about the hurts of life—yet overwhelmingly full of hope about the God who gives life. A great encouragement to women who are suffering.

**THEGOODBOOK.COM/HOPE**
**THEGOODBOOK.CO.UK/HOPE**

# thegoodbook
## COMPANY

**BIBLICAL | RELEVANT | ACCESSIBLE**

At The Good Book Company, we are dedicated to helping Christians and local churches grow. We believe that God's growth process always starts with hearing clearly what he has said to us through his timeless word—the Bible.

Ever since we opened our doors in 1991, we have been striving to produce resources that honor God in the way the Bible is used. We have grown to become an international provider of user-friendly resources to the Christian community, with believers of all backgrounds and denominations using our Bible studies, books, evangelistic resources, DVD-based courses, and training events.

We want to equip ordinary Christians to live for Christ day by day, and churches to grow in their knowledge of God, their love for one another, and the effectiveness of their outreach.

Call us for a discussion of your needs or visit one of our local websites for more information on the resources and services we provide.

Your friends at The Good Book Company

---

**NORTH AMERICA**
**UK & EUROPE**
**AUSTRALIA**
**NEW ZEALAND**

 thegoodbook.com
thegoodbook.co.uk
thegoodbook.com.au
thegoodbook.co.nz

 866 244 2165
0333 123 0880
(02) 9564 3555
(+64) 3 343 2463

 **WWW.CHRISTIANITYEXPLORED.ORG**
Our partner site is a great place for those exploring the Christian faith, with a clear explanation of the good news, powerful testimonies and answers to difficult questions.